CONSEQUENCES

A pensive moment in autumn, my favorite season.
(© *Sherman Hines*)

MARGARET TRUDEAU

CONSEQUENCES

A Seal Book
Distributed by
The Canadian Publishers
McClelland and Stewart Limited
25 Hollinger Road, Toronto M4B 3G2

Canadian Cataloguing in Publication Data

Trudeau, Margaret, 1948 –
  Consequences

ISBN 0-7704-01850-3

1. Trudeau, Margaret, 1948 –   2. Prime ministers —
  Canada — Spouses — Biography. I. Title.

FC626.T78A32   971.064′4′0924   C82-094091-4

F1034.3.T78A32

Cover photo by Anthony Loew.

The excerpt on page 147 is from MAGGIE & PIERRE, Copyright © 1980 by Linda Griffiths with Paul Thompson. Reprinted courtesy of Talonbooks.

Once again, to Caroline Moorehead, who with tape recorder and typewriter helped me face the consequences.

THE PRICE YOU PAY

You make up your mind, you choose the chance you
   take
You ride to where the highway ends and the desert
   breaks
Out on to an open road you ride until the day
You learn to sleep at night with the price you pay

So let the game start, you better run you little wild heart
You can run through all the nights and all the days
But just across the country line, a stranger passing
   through put up a sign
That counts the men fallen away to the price you pay,
   and girl before the end of the day,
I'm gonna tear it down and throw it away

CONTENTS

Chapter One
The Prime Minister's Wife

I was twenty-two when I married the Prime Minister of
Canada, Pierre Trudeau. I was twenty-eight when we
publicly separated, mother by then of three small sons,
Justin, Sacha and Michel. But I was almost thirty before
we made a truly clean break in November 1979, and
those months in between were not for the most part
glorious ones. There were many Canadians who condemned my much publicized comings and goings as the
behaviour of someone who preferred the pleasures of
international high society to the duties of being a Prime
Minister's wife, someone who was willing to sacrifice her
children to ambition. A few people wrote to tell me that
they admired me for my independence and my courage.
Many more considered me willful and destructive.

I first set eyes on Pierre in Tahiti, the Christmas of
1967. I was lazing on a raft out at sea off the coast of
Moorea when a man whose skill at water skiing I had
been admiring came over to talk to me. We idled the
afternoon away on student politics and Plato. Only that
evening did I learn that the stranger was Pierre Trudeau,
black sheep of the federal Liberal Party. He struck me as
old and square.

Many months were to pass before we met again. I
spent the time turning into a flower child in Morocco,

flirting with drugs, frizzing my hair, experimenting with macrobiotic diets and enraging my somewhat domineering father, James Sinclair, a former cabinet minister with the federal Liberals, and my long-suffering mother, Kathleen, while my four sisters looked on with disbelief. It was in this condition, rebellious, hippie and self-obsessed, that Pierrre found me when he invited me out for our first date in August 1969. In the total secrecy that surrounded our meetings I then set out to learn the things that were important to him: I studied French, became a Catholic and practised my skiing.

I look back on those months now with incredulity, the way I kept up a pretence that I was not even seeing Pierre, so that the day we married only my immediate family knew that the room booked for a dinner at the Capilano Golf and Country Club in my hometown, Vancouver, was not a Sinclair family celebration but a wedding feast.

Pierre took a risk when he married me on the chilly spring evening of March 4, 1971. Despite my year's preparations, I was not the most natural wife for a distinguished politician, a clearheaded man who lived by iron discipline and work. But then I took a risk too. Pierre was fifty-one – twenty-nine years older than I. He was truly adult while I still had everything to discover. What little I had seen of official life, the social functions, the ever-present security guards, the horrible political dimensions of events like the separatist kidnappings of James Cross and Pierre Laporte, I had shied away from with extreme misgivings.

Both of us thought we could work it out. Pierre wanted a wife, a companion to transform the gloom of the Prime Minister's residence, 24 Sussex Drive, and the solitude of his empty evenings. I wanted the excitement and fun of being with him. It was only later that I came to understand that Pierre didn't really need me, only the

10

image of someone I was not, while for me the pleasure soon vanished beneath a crushing blanket of protocol. I was being forced to be a matron before my time.

It was never easy being the Prime Minister's wife. From the first day I came to 24 Sussex, I found the trappings of a grand life, the servants and the austere official surroundings claustrophobic. I did my best to improve the decor of the house, as well as the country residence at Harrington Lake, and I believe that there I succeeded, just as I had some success at recruiting a team of people to work for us and run the Prime Minister's establishment with great efficiency. It was the one job that Pierre let me perform, and it did much to check, for the first few years at least, a growing uncertainty about my own identity and purpose in his life. When that was completed, there was nothing left for me to do, nothing to halt a confused descent into self-doubt.

For there my troubles really started. While I successfully played the role of everybody's darling, charming geriatric senators and political pundits, I felt lost without a realistic role of my own. I made gaffes with foreign dignitaries, doing things impetuously that I thought would be well received, only to have them thrown in my face as tactless. One time I was ridiculed for singing a personal aria of thanks to Venezuela's first lady, Mme Blanquita Pérez. Another time I unwittingly shocked a roomful of dignitaries by wearing a calf-length, rather than a full-length, dress to the White House on a formal visit to Washington. I fought with the servants and chafed at the security men, coming to see them with time more as jailers than protectors.

And, strongest of all perhaps, I hated being a public figure. I hated being recognized wherever I went. I hated the way people felt they owned me, so that they could comment on my actions and beliefs with impunity as rudely and critically as they wished. I felt constantly

11

under observation of the harshest and least forgiving kind. I realize now that much of my more extravagant behaviour was due to a desire to fight back, to prove that I was a person and not an object, but the harder I fought and the more outrageous I became, the more hostile grew the watching public.

It became harder and harder to remember that, for a brief, dazzling period, Pierre and I had fun. We were happy. Even during the bad spells, whenever we were able to re-create the privacy and innocence of our early secret life, we flourished. My sons were part of this cocoon of happiness. Justin was born on Christmas Day 1971, to the warmth and appreciation of the Canadian people, who inundated us with booties and handknitted sweaters. Two years later to the day came Sacha, a second Christmas baby, and less than two years after that came Michel, whom we called Micha for short. Together, united in the intimacy that only the most extreme formal life creates, we made marvellous trips – to Cuba to stay with Fidel Castro, to China to see Chou En-lai, to Rome for an audience with Pope Paul VI. These were the good moments.

But as Pierre's wife I failed. I did not have enough confidence in us to sustain the dream, nor the discipline to see it through. And Pierre's nature was such that he wasn't able to help me, so as I sank into greater confusion he, like the Canadian public, grew increasingly disapproving. The account of how I struggled to make our marriage work and to perform my official obligations, but in the end could bear that world no longer, is contained in my first book, *Beyond Reason*. "I don't, I realize, come out of this story very well," I wrote at the time. "I have tried at least to be honest."

Those words brought me friends. Just as the public had responded during the winter of 1974 when the pressures of my life had driven me into a psychiatric hospital for help, so people now came forward, after my book

12

appeared in Canada in April 1979, to tell me that they were behind me. Strangers who had once condemned my behaviour as flighty now wrote to tell me that they appreciated my honesty, even if they could not applaud what I had done. That did a lot for my self-esteem. For years I had been under constant, unrelenting criticism. Now, being truthful, I was praised. It gave me hope.

I needed it. The aftermath of my marriage sent me on a downward spiral of exploration and adventure. I seized on people, on jobs, on drugs, avidly, with desperation. Each let me down. I seemed to have no sense of the weight or worth of anything. Often, there were days when I truly did not see how I could carry on. During those times I realized that the years of my marriage to Pierre had been the easy ones, even if we were rarely perfectly happy, even if we often fought and did our best to destroy one another. The country house at the lake, the maids, the security men, the absolute certainty that my three boys were going to be clothed, fed and brought up properly – those were the secure times.

What befell me when I parted from Pierre in the spring of 1977 was far worse. I embarked on a long spell of double life, married to Pierre in name, yet at the same time distanced from him to the point of mutual cruelty. I was of course free at last to do anything I wanted, and yet I felt more trapped than ever, since he kept the boys. I was in a position to go wherever I wanted but there was nowhere I could go, since Pierre would give me no money, and I was too proud to turn to my parents for help.

I believe, I hope, that all that is now past. I have a new life, a new understanding with Pierre and, what is most important of all, a system of raising our children both of us believe to be the right one. We are co-parents, sharing every decision that concerns our sons. We have them on alternating weeks, and we like each other as parents.

I hope, too, that if I describe the past years, tell of some of the things I did, some of the risks I took to secure a new life, that I might be of help to others who, like me, are fighting confusion and self-doubt. Others who feel the urgent need to design their own life pattern – one in which others do not dictate or dominate and in which there is neither oppression nor exploitation.

Once again, I don't have much to boast about. Once again I have tried to be honest.

Being a chatelaine before a reception at 24 Sussex. *(Bill Brennan)*

The dining room was such an elegant, rich room before the
rapid renovations of Ms McTeer. *(Bill Brennan)*

Discussing menus with the chef, Yannick Vincent.
(Bill Brennan)

Supervising the table setting with Hildegarde West.
(Bill Brennan)

Lucky mummy with her three bonnie lads.
(Bill Brennan)

Justin tries out the new camera.
(Courtesy Margaret Trudeau)

A spring day at 24 Sussex.
(Bill Brennan)

King Hussein and Princess Alia.
(Courtesy Margaret Trudeau)

With Liza Minnelli at Studio 54. *(Wide World Photos)*

My friend Gro Southam meets me in Ottawa. *(Bill Brennan)*

On my first photographic assignment in France, Bruce Nevins was my charming subject.
(Courtesy Margaret Trudeau)

Just before they shout "Action" on the set of KINGS AND DESPERATE MEN.

It was an honour to
photograph one of my
favorite Canadians,
Karen Kain.
(Courtesy Margaret Trudeau)

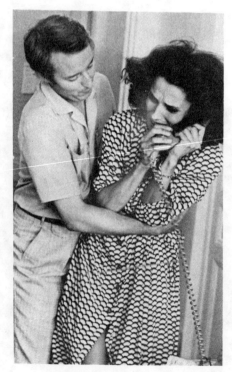

I play the mistress of a
wealthy industrialist in THE
GUARDIAN ANGEL.

Chapter Two
The High Life

In the late spring of 1977, I decided, after many hours of agonizing, to choose independence over my marital vows. By then about two years had passed since I first realized that this was not the life for me, two years during which I had gone to bed at night whispering to myself, "Pierre, please give me a divorce," but never daring to say the words aloud.

Pierre's reaction to my flight was calm. He was sad, but he was accepting. There was no anger, no muddle and no strain. All that was temporarily behind us. He knew the reality – more than I did perhaps because he was so much more mature than I was. But he too had come to see that the moment had really arrived for me to leave (in his words, to "search for my own truth") and that this situation was part of my growing-up process. It might even, he hoped, be my way back to him.

We said nothing to the boys. Justin was just six, Sacha four and Michel barely two: we told them that I was going to look for work and would come home as often as I could. They accepted it.

To the rest of the world, my fresh departure from 24 Sussex was nothing more than another "freedom trip," a custom Pierre and I had laughingly instituted in the early days of our marriage when it became obvious that I needed to escape the hated claustrophobia of official life. Usually I made these journeys for two or three weeks at a time with family or close friends to places where few people knew or cared who I was. "Mrs Trudeau flies to New York." So what? She'd done that before.

The first year of my separation was not a year I am proud of. I filled the time with aimless comings and goings, breakdowns, and getting into publicity scrapes that affected not just my standing in Canada but Pierre's whole political future. I was caught up in a scandal involving Rolling Stones leader Mick Jagger; made many trips, not all of them respectable. I took acting classes and became a photographer; formed close relationships only to see them vanish again. A lot of experiences were crammed into that year, and I talked about many of them in *Beyond Reason*. I'm not going to tell them again.

What I was after, primarily, was economic stability of my own, for Pierre, so loving and understanding in many ways, has one blind spot: he is mean about money. As long as I stayed at 24 Sussex, the bills would be paid. For everything else – clothes, trips with friends, the money to launch a career – I was on my own. I had been begging him for a long time to give me just enough money to buy a small red brick house where I could raise my sons and have what every other wife and mother has: her own home. It wasn't that I didn't like 24 Sussex Drive, just that I felt a prisoner there, a visitor with no authority and no freedom. I didn't necessarily even wish to abandon our marriage for good, but Pierre was so jealous that he thought he was being asked to finance a love nest.

Once the decision to take off was made, I felt sudden, overwhelming relief, even exhilaration. But behind it, I also felt deep anxiety, a tremulous sort of fear and doubt that I could actually make it on my own. I have always been very good at hiding everything that goes on inside

24

me, however, and so I pushed firmly below my consciousness any suggestion that I was refusing to face up to my failures – to Pierre, my marriage or my children.

Instead I decided that, since the children were being well cared for at 24 Sussex by reliable and loving nannies, I would now concentrate, entirely selfishly, on myself, my wellbeing and my future. My quest was to find myself, to get back to the old me, the one I used to like before the years of officialdom had broken me down. When I found her, perhaps then I could come home in peace.

And so I set off to make my fortune, through work or friends, on what turned out to be the greatest freedom trip of all. That such freedom is illusory was a lesson I was to learn only much later. I thought it was for good. It lasted a couple of months.

My first stop was New York, where I had heard there might be work among a group of good photographers I knew. I also had an apartment waiting for me: a friend from Houston had asked me to house-sit in a largely unfurnished luxury apartment on Park Avenue until the decorators moved in.

I loved New York. I had many friends, I had my favourite night spot, Studio 54, and for the first several months I had the perfect companion – Bruce Nevins, the French bottled water millionaire whom even his friends called "Mr Perrier." Bruce was handsome, warm, loving... but he also turned out to be a confirmed bachelor, and I cared too much for him to put up with it. So I moved on, and soon found a new man, Tommy, a Texan cowboy complete with high-heeled boots and hat.

One April morning in 1978, almost a year after I first left Pierre, I received a phone call from an American publisher based in London, John Marqusee of Paddington Press. "Are you interested in writing your memoirs?" he asked. John wanted to fly me to London on Concorde, pay all my expenses and discuss a deal. I packed my bags and set out to have a look at what was offered.

John met me at the airport. I looked around the Concorde lounge and saw a square, paunchy man with clean-cut looks. He came up to me. The posture was undeniably English – tweed suit, a little hat – but the accent was unmistakably American. "Are you on the pill?" he asked, by way of introduction. Even I thought this was fast going. It turned out later that he had noticed me smoking and that he knew that the combination of smoking and being on the pill could lead to blood-clotting problems. But it was a curious introduction, and the trendy, know-all familiarity should have warned me.

The Marqusees could not do enough for me: limousines at the airport, a fine hotel, expensive restaurants and, above all, admiration. I began to feel good: the author at work. I returned to New York with the agreement signed.

I was way past caution. I didn't stop long to think what sort of public effect I might make with my stories, and in any case John cleverly persuaded me that my book would be not sordid revelations but a document of considerable contemporary historical importance – a sort of modern commentary on society. And a book meant money – I called it my alimony as justification – to go back to Ottawa and buy the home that Pierre would not give me, where I could raise my three boys. What was more, it meant escape from New York, where I seemed to be sinking lower and lower in a world that appeared to have no bottom.

In May I went back to London. This time Tommy was with me, though we stayed in different hotels: he at Brown's, I at the Montcalm. Tommy had possessed, before I knew him, the looks of a Greek god: tall, forceful and exceedingly handsome. Then one day he and his

26

uncle had been flying in a small plane over the jungle in Colombia when the jet had crashed, severely burning his face and hands, leaving his face vulnerably patched up with grafted skin, and one hand so disfigured that he had to wear a leather glove. What had drawn me to him in the first place was his extreme youth – he was just twenty-three – and the way both of us shared the fact that we had been badly hurt, he with his physical burns, me with my mental ones from Pierre and the media.

He represented something new for me: as a rock musician he was offering me a glimpse of another culture, one laced with drugs and sex, just at a time when I was looking for ways of escaping the increasingly painful reality of having left Pierre. I was lonely and I felt broke, and here was this lean, rich, muscular, sexy cowboy, a romantic wounded rebel, a medieval cavalier, who was going to sweep me off my feet and carry me away into a better sunset.

Then began a new phase of high life. It wasn't New York nightclubs like Studio 54, with the amyl nitrate, the lost days, the Halstons and Andy Warhols and Truman Capotes. But it wasn't much better. I thought I had left drugs behind me in the States. I found they had followed me to London. Around Tommy there circled a sad and sleazy mob of jet-setters, avid for the parties yet more avid for their drugs. Night after night I found myself in elegant Belgravia penthouses watching the lineups form outside the bathrooms, people waiting to get in there and have a snort. I had tried to stop using drugs but it wasn't always easy when I felt so uncertain that I was doing the right thing with my life and could see other people stumble into a bathroom only to emerge minutes later euphoric, bouncy and full of confidence. I didn't always keep my head.

There were many times when I would have liked to blame all my mistakes on cocaine. That way I could have eased my conscience. I can't, in all truth, do that. But I can say that cocaine is a very costly social drug. It had a terrible, negative effect on my life. The abuse of it not only debilitated me physically, in that I got extremely thin and tense, but it also created in me a sensation of hostility and paranoia, and made me say things, particularly when I was back in Ottawa with Pierre, that I would never normally have said to anyone. I found it made me boastful, obnoxious and argumentative. What was so seductive about it, after I had been on it for a while, was its secretive side compared to marijuana, which makes the room reek. But it was its insidious accessibility that was to be my downfall. I soon found that I had no difficulty getting it, no matter where I was.

I now believe that my indulgence in cocaine was the start of a myth about me that later grew out of all proportion: that I was a manic depressive. With the coke, I took Valium... coke to get me up, Valium to bring me down again. Only Valium did more than bring me down. It made me low and depressed – far lower and more depressed than I had ever been naturally – so that I actually *needed* the cocaine to become exuberant and euphoric once more. Rather than work out my inner rage, therefore, I preferred to resort to these artificial highs and lows, taking ever more of each to acquire some sort of balance. Later, when I told the doctors it was not me who was manic depressive but what I did to myself that made me appear so, no one would listen.

Life with Tommy was exhilarating, but it didn't help my stability. He liked to stay up all night eating caviar and drinking champagne, then sleep through the day. I didn't always have the stamina to keep up with him. One night we had been out dining with friends. To me, the evening seemed finished around midnight and I longed to sleep, so I crept into Tommy's bed in his suite at Brown's while the others kept drinking in the room next door. Toward dawn, I was shaken awake:

28

"Come on Maggie, wake up. We want food."

I groaned. "Try room service."

He laughed. "That's just it: Brown's won't do all-night room service. The Montcalm will. We're all going over there."

I protested.

"Well, if you're not going to come, we're going anyway." Then Tommy added, with a touch of menace, "You get up, woman."

Realizing that disaster lay that way, I dressed, silently furious, and led the party back to the Montcalm. Though not exactly pleased to see us, the management agreed to send up to my room the bottles of Scotch, rye and vodka and the six steaks that Tommy ordered. As for myself, I dragged the blankets off my bed and curled up in the bathtub. Room service came but so did the bill: two hundred pounds.

Tommy's attitude to money dazzled me. He kept his jeans pockets full of hundred-dollar bills, which he would drag out whenever he needed cash, scattering money. Everywhere he went, he saw things he wanted. When he moved into his suite at Brown's, he decided that he didn't like the radio, so he went out and bought a stereo, complete with amplifiers and speakers, for five hundred pounds. He was only staying a few weeks.

The spending was infectious and also, it later turned out, ruinous. We had endless champagne, more caviar than I could eat, and when it was my hotel it was I who paid. "I'll take care of you, darlin'," Tommy used to say, but the offer carried the threat: "I'll make you do what *I* want." In any case, I wasn't broke. The Marqusees were only too pleased to keep me in funds, pressing envelopes of ten-pound notes into my hands whenever I asked for them, anything to keep me sweet.

Fired by Tommy's example, eager to emulate the flashy friends with whom I now spent my time, and more than anything intoxicated with my newfound spending power, I went on stupendous shopping sprees. All was now going my way: I had reached easy street – why not dress for the part? An average day took me to South Molton Street to browse through Brown's, wonder whether I felt like a Chloë suit or an Ungaro coat, then on to Bond Street. Did I need some shoes from Charles Jourdan? A silk dress from Yves St Laurent? Perhaps a watch from Aspreys? I thought nothing of spending two thousand pounds on an outing. Sure, I was being spendthrift; sure, I hadn't actually *earned* the money yet, but wasn't I working hard on my book?

When I wasn't staying in fancy hotels – I soon moved to the Savoy for the London trips – or eating at the Connaught (not that I did much eating, with the result that I was fast becoming emaciated), I was crossing the Atlantic on Concorde. There is nothing like Concorde for the ritzy life. I didn't even bat an eye when on one trip I found ex-Beatle Ringo Starr across the aisle and tennis star Jimmy Connors directly behind me. Wasn't I part of the Concorde set? What no one ever told me was that anyone can buy a ticket for Concorde. Nor that all this money wasn't exactly a present; it was coming directly from the would-be profits of the book.

Not long after our arrival in London, Tommy and I had bumped into Mark Shand, a charming bachelor who soon won me over with his boyish, athletic looks, the twinkle in his eye, and his ineffable roguish gallantry. He was a latter-day Errol Flynn who had a house in Bali and made his money as an art dealer, selling his rich friends little Fabergé eggs which he would carry around in his pockets. Mark was not my lover – he was more like a charming leading man and he had great class. I never got over the day when he arrived to pick me up with his Range Rover covered in peacock droppings from the birds that roamed the gardens of his country home.

It was Mark who introduced me to the Summers.

30

Martin and Nona Summers are the deans of the international jet set in London. When I first met them, they were still in the honeymoon days of their marriage, and from the start I admired and envied their relationship, the way they treated each other so well and so lovingly. Martin was the prototype of the understated English aristocrat: articulate, elegant and decent. Nona, his second wife, was his exact opposite. Tousled and red-haired, eccentric and worldly, she seemed bent on transforming his sober life into an exotic feast of parties. Nona had a huge heart, but she also had a delightfully wicked streak to her: she liked to matchmake and observe and cause things to happen around her. More than anything else, she liked parties and she liked to have fun.

The more disenchanted I grew with Tommy and his macho ways, the more anxious I was to spend time with the Summers. They had a style I found irresistible, a flair for having fun that didn't seem to depend on drugs. They had each other, they had money and friends, and they both worked hard: she as a freelance contributor on fashion and society for *Town and Country* magazine, he as a curator at the Lefèvre Gallery on New Bond Street. How could I not envy them?

I spent many evenings in their company, revelling in exciting and enjoyable dinner parties of the kind I had always believed I would have with Pierre but never did, parties attended by the best actors, the best sculptors, the best writers. Sometimes I did the cooking, like the night when Superman, Christopher Reeve, came to dinner and I made lamb rolled in herbs with a cucumber and yogurt sauce only to find that he wouldn't eat because he had flu (Superman with flu?) and preferred to go and watch himself on a recorded talk show on television. Other times I listened to the marvellous conversations around me, or laughed at stories such as the one told to me by Franco Rossellini, co-producer of the film

Caligula, about him sending writer Gore Vidal an ornate Florentine box full of horse manure after Vidal had slammed the production in the press.

The high life was explosive, and funny, and it never seemed to stop. One night after a concert by Bob Dylan, Nona, who had known Bob for some time, invited him to bring back a few friends for a drink. We expected half a dozen people, no more. At about eleven, the doorbell rang and when Martin went to answer it no less than thirty-five people trooped in. Bob had brought his roadies, his technicians, his whole band – in fact, he had hired a bus to do so. They descended on the house like locusts and before long Nona (by now in a rage) and I were reduced to combing through old airline bags for unused little sample bottles of Courvoisier. For, locust-like, they had stripped the house bare of all liquor.

The women who attended the Summers' parties had to be pretty: that was the rule. Youth, sexiness, availability. The same pretty young things cropped up at every party with a different man, always laughing, always there. Nona, in her leopard skintight polyester pants and crazy T-shirts, was the star of the show, and there wasn't an evening that didn't include celebrities such as Bianca Jagger, Stavros Niarchos' sons Phillipe and Spiro, and just about every movie star on location in London.

I felt as if I were just coming out of a musty cedar closet. Pierre had always made it clear that I was only of interest as his wife. He was being proved wrong. Nona brought out the best in me: she was far more outrageous, alive and wild than I had ever dared to be and I was soon swept away in an enthusiasm for life.

Of all the people I bumped into with the Summers, Bianca Jagger was certainly the one least pleased to see me. I never found her easy to get along with after my Rolling Stones escapade the previous year in Toronto.

Friends assured me that Mick had told her there had been nothing between us, but she just took the line that I had publicly cuckolded her.

There was more to it than that, however. We had one thing in common – our public notoriety – and I kept feeling that it was sad that we couldn't get beyond the feminine jealousy. After all, we were on much the same quest, that of escape from our past. She just wanted to erase hers, as if it had never taken place, but I knew better than anyone that you can't do that, you have to live with what's gone before. Mick had saved her from an impoverished Latin American childhood; Pierre had saved me, from what? Perhaps mediocrity. We were now both looking for something. But what?

At the same time, I couldn't help feeling a bit envious. Unlike me, Bianca had lots of money. In London she lived a very indulgent life with servants and the most outrageously expensive and unusual clothes. She made the most of it all. Still, I thought sometimes when I watched her preposterous behaviour that her chances of survival were as limited as my own.

Behind the fun, I felt lost. However hard I looked for them, I couldn't find any roots. The parties and the people did a lot for me: they taught me that I could stand on my own feet again. But alone with myself late at night or first thing in the morning I cried. All of my guilt and recrimination at my excessive lifestyle would surface. I thought about the boys. I missed them terribly, and I worried about all the things, however small, that might be happening to them while I was not there to comfort them. The nannies might be angry, or Pierre too strict. "I should be there, I should be there," kept going through my head.

And so the fun paled; I couldn't seem to attach much importance to any of it. Every couple of weeks, having convinced myself that my heart lay in Ottawa, I would dash home again, fantasizing about Pierre waiting for me with open arms only to find him the same as ever, busy, detached, rather disapproving. My fantasy brutally dispelled, I would turn around and join the party set once more. Nona got it right when she said to someone: "That's Margaret for you. Now you see her, now you don't." Because I would come into their world, become involved, then be gone again.

Also, I was beginning to feel bitter. The life my new friends lived was overwhelmingly secure: they had one another and they had money and yet they were also intelligent, responsible people. I couldn't prevent myself from feeling relatively deprived – some part of me has always wanted to be super-rich, to own twenty-nine pairs of shoes and drive a Bentley.

So I started to resent Pierre, his money and his meanness, the way he seemed to have taken the children. Moving between Ottawa and London, between domesticity and parties, I grew increasingly hostile and paranoid and a huge rage built up inside me. My physical health was rapidly deteriorating. I was troubled by headaches and an ulcer, and it got so bad that there was almost nothing I could eat without pain. In my misery I began to convince myself that Pierre had pushed me out, that he wanted me gone, dead. With this came a terrible sense of hurt, a feeling that I had lost the best things in my life.

That summer of 1978, Nona and Martin moved into a new house. It was to be the pleasure palace of the movie world. Four townhouses converted into one, built around an immense central drawing room draped with Eastern cloth to form a vast Arabian tent, the inside decorated with priceless hangings. Above, an enormous skylight with swishing, electronically controlled curtains let in muted daylight, so that the effect was one of a pasha's sumptuous palace. Exquisite bronzes and ceramics were dotted around on ormolu tables; flowering shrubs and full-sized palms lent their aura of the East; a splendid and faultless stereo murmured soothing sounds of romance and ballad. Never had I seen such an exotic and enticing place. It has become more remarkable since. Martin is a talented gardener and he has covered the roof with hundreds of plants and flowers – all of them pink.

Just before they moved in, the Summers had one final party at their old apartment. Lots of people were there: Terence Stamp, Margot Kidder – all the beautiful people. So was Jack Nicholson. He was alone, and I took to him at once: the leering twinkle in his eyes, the quizzical smile familiar to me from dozens of viewings of his films.

After dinner the Summers suggested going dancing at a disco called Tramps. By then I had formed a plan: I was going to get to know Jack Nicholson. But how to get rid of Tommy? Nona and I conferred. She joined the others. "Let's go," she said, stirring them all out of their seats, busily deciding who should go with whom, which cars to take. It was done in a flash. Jack and I hid in the kitchen until they were gone, assuming that in the confusion no one would notice our absence.

For a while the plan worked.

We heard the last taxi rumble away down the street, crept out, and raced over to the new house. It was still half-finished at that point, except for the drawing room, where the tent hung waiting for us, above down-filled sofas. We made our way there, taking a bottle of wine from a providential supply in the hall.

I can't really remember now what we talked about, but it was rapidly becoming clear to me that Jack was perhaps the first real rival to Pierre I had ever come across, a decent, inquiring man who could make me

35

laugh. This was an exciting moment. Until then, no matter how hard I looked, I had never met a man whom I thought could ever take Pierre's place.

I liked his good manners, his soft, slow voice. So I didn't listen too closely when he told me – with extreme scrupulousness – about the woman he loved, actress Angelica Huston, who was about to join him in London. Far too soon there were furious bangs on the outer door. Reluctantly, Jack went to answer. It was Tommy. I went quietly.

A couple of nights later other friends invited about twenty of us to a Russian restaurant where they had reserved a bright-red private dining room in the basement. There were blintzes and caviar and a great deal of vodka. Jack was there and soon we were settled into a bantering and highly pleasurable sort of flirting. Matters were fast becoming plain to me: Tommy was making me feel claustrophobic – and I wanted Jack.

Then began a mad episode that took us roaring around London in the early hours of the morning. Saying I wanted some fresh air, I was leaving to go into the street when Jack suggested that I should sit in his Daimler, parked outside, with his driver George. Once outside, we plotted: Jack was to go back in and say that he had asked his driver to take me back to the Montcalm as I was feeling ill. George would then circle the block and when the others had finally left we would return, pick up Jack, and speed off.

We hadn't reckoned with Tommy. He and Jack came out together. From the spot where we were hiding down the street, I could see Jack making frantic signs with his arms to denote hopeless confusion. The two men hailed a taxi, climbed in, and as it passed our parking space I crouched down on the floor to escape detection. George pulled the Daimler out and we set off in pursuit.

To my relief, Jack soon dropped Tommy off at Brown's

Hotel, gave him a chance to vanish through the swinging doors, paid off the taxi and joined us. That night, driving around London behind the inscrutable George, I discovered just how much room there is in the back of a Daimler.

From then on, I spent a lot of time with Jack. He was in London to make *The Shining* and spent his days on location, but each evening he was back in London where he had rented a terrace house in Cheyne Walk, one of the city's finest streets, overlooking the Thames.

After the night of the Daimler, Tommy had taken the hint, packed his bags and gone. I had quite simply outgrown him, become disillusioned with my would-be cowboy without a horse. He had given me a great deal. He had made me feel young and sexy once more, made me put the matronly blues behind me and realize that it is better to be young and make mistakes and face them than become bitter. But as has happened so often with me, I had expected too much of him, and our moment was now past.

Before meeting Jack, I had been miserably bothered by reporters. There was nowhere I could go without being pestered for a photograph or an interview. I refused them all, hoping that they would grow bored with my presence, hoping that on one of my return trips there would be no eager mob as I stepped out of the Concorde, but I never had much luck. It may have been what I now see as my silly and provocative behaviour that made them keep coming – such as the time I insisted on riding along the back window ledge of a car on the way home from a party, or the crazy hours at which I left and returned to my hotel.

But Jack was obsessed with discretion, and under his tuition I learned how to move more calmly and less publicly through the streets of London. Most evenings we stayed at his house, occasionally we joined friends to go to the movies, and once he took me to a screening of his new movie, *Goin' South*.

One night, having forgotten his keys, Jack pulled himself onto the high wall that surrounded his garden and jumped down into the courtyard. Falling, he injured his back. It wasn't serious, but it was enough to keep him lying on his back for a few days, stretched out on a chaise longue in the drawing room, holding court for his friends, all interesting, clever people from a world I warmed to.

It was at one of these gatherings that I heard the story of Frances Farmer, a sort of female version of the man Jack had played in *One Flew Over the Cuckoo's Nest*, and swore that I would, some day, play her part in the film. The grande dame of American fashion, Diana Vreeland, was spending the evening with us and she and Jack talked about what a beautiful bright actress Frances Farmer was in the Forties, much dominated by a tyrannical mother who wanted her to be a great star. One night Frances Farmer was picked up for drunken driving and, to avoid a jail sentence, agreed to plead temporary insanity, her mother becoming her "conservator." A year or so later, wanting to leave movies and go into politics, she found herself committed to a mental asylum by her mother. She underwent a lobotomy and finally committed suicide.

I felt a great deal of empathy with Frances Farmer. She had suffered because she was too intelligent and too feminine and beautiful. I felt the same thing happened in my life. I knew I had always been too cute for my own good, too sexy, that I could always get what I wanted, and yet my intelligence forced me to see that it's not enough to be prom queen. You have to get top marks as well.

Frances Farmer's story was also very romantic. She

38

was a leading lady in the heyday of Hollywood. But that wasn't what she wanted. She had an active, well-tutored mind that kept getting in the way of allowing herself to be treated like a sex object. And when she became demented, I thought I knew how she felt, the rage, the bitterness, the feeling of "why me?" I could see myself as Frances Farmer or as Saint Joan, or as any one of the tragic heroines, because I see myself as a tragic person.

All this time I was trying not to think about Angelica. Each day I awoke to hear Jack on the telephone ordering another two dozen red roses or an arum lily to be delivered to the home they shared in Los Angeles, and every day or so he would tell me she was just about to arrive. Every day, though, I felt myself becoming more involved with him. I loved the fight in him, his passion for work, his caustic humour and the way he made me laugh.

He reminded me of Pierre. Pierre has tremendous moral dedication to his country; Jack has the same kind of dedication, but to a world that I felt myself much more drawn to, a world of movie stars and Rolls-Royces and good conversation and fine acting. He was the first man who even held a candle to Pierre Trudeau and I was desperately looking for a way of getting that man out of my life.

I also felt bewitched by Jack: there is something slightly demonic about him, both strong and tender, and something enormously attractive about his success. I didn't know whether I had it in my power to make him happy, but I was beginning to sense that he had it in his power to make me content.

In July 1978, when I returned to London from a visit home, Jack seemed pleased to see me but was quick to tell me that he had just bought a Toulouse-Lautrec for Angelica's birthday on the tenth, by which time he confidently expected her to arrive in London. The days went by. One brought a telegram saying that she had decided instead to go to Ireland to sing ballads with Art Garfunkel. Jack was furious. "I didn't know *she* could sing."

One warm summer's night I arrived at his place for our usual date. We had dinner, talked. Later, Jack said, almost casually, "Angelica is coming tomorrow." I had half-expected it, of course, but that didn't stop the sudden stab of despair. I felt instantly crushed. I felt a fool. I had almost managed to convince myself that his supposed love for Angelica was a convenience to protect him from his many female admirers and that eventually I could work my way into his heart. That I was so wrong was one more blow, reinforcing Pierre's bitter words about people using me, about how I would never find happiness with another man, that I was too immature, too narcissistic to have a true relationship with anyone. He had said it, and now I was tempted to agree: I was doomed. I felt unsteady on my feet.

We made love all night. In the morning Jack went to work and I returned to the Savoy. The episode had shaken me, but I was not broken. For one thing, I was making good progress on my book. For another, I knew he liked me, and since we hadn't actually been living together there wasn't that pain, that hole of separation. I wanted him badly. But I didn't *need* him. All that happened was that I now felt worse about myself.

I didn't see Jack again. But I did see Angelica. One of the humiliations about having her in town was that I was banned from the parties they attended together. Even Nona wasn't above phoning me and saying, "Do you want to come over tonight? Jack can't make it," only to call back a little later and say, "Sorry, darling, Jack can make it now. I'm sure you'll understand. . . ."

Just before I was due to leave, I got another call from Nona; this time the invitation wasn't cancelled before I could turn up. I spent a somewhat desultory early part of the evening, having come for the purpose of catching a glimpse of the fabulous Angelica who was rumoured to be there on her own, since Jack was filming. After a boring half-hour sitting on the famous down-filled sofa between two rather leaden, plain women, I muttered something about needing a drink and went in search of Nona.

"Where is Angelica, for heaven's sake? Is she *never* coming?"

Nona looked about her, laughing. "She's there," she said, pointing to the larger, more hippy of my two companions on the sofa.

Where was the beauty with the long raven tresses? The magical temptress with the charms of a Helen of Troy? Because of my love for Jack I had endowed Angelica in my mind with every feminine quality a woman could possess. Because her father was director and actor John Huston, ever my hero, I had imagined a witty, flawless paragon. Instead I saw before me a big horsey girl with short-cropped hair, an aquiline nose and a hard and hearty look. I just couldn't see in her my rival. Later, of course, I came to see what a fine girl she is, and feel ashamed of my jealous thoughts.

That night I met Jorge, a Peruvian racing driver. He took me to dine with friends in Belgravia, then on to Tramps where he fed me champagne and dropped me, with evident admiration but no advances, at the Savoy. Next morning, twelve long-stemmed pink roses were outside my door. How easily I made friends, I thought, and how very painfully I parted from them. I determined to put aside my feelings about Jack, to stay on in London and enjoy myself without him. But I had become a little more jaded, more impatient. I still managed to have good times, but they came less frequently. There was no denying my dissatisfaction.

Then, one October weekend, Sabrina Guinness (a

former girlfriend of Prince Charles), Nona and I were invited to spend a high society weekend in Paris. Valentino, from whom I had purchased my first couture dress, was hosting a gala evening at the ballet – Mikhail Baryshnikov in *Queen of Hearts* – followed by a dinner party at Maxim's. The most dazzling lights in fashion were to be there.

We were brought over from London and put up in a luxurious big suite at the Maurice to add glitter to the occasion – but nobody expected that we'd outshine all the other luminaries. From the moment we arrived the paparazzi went wild. They swarmed all over us, leaving everyone else feeling terribly neglected, with the result that people blamed *me* for attracting so much attention.

Had it not been for the graciousness of Pierre Cardin, I'd have come away from my weekend in Paris badly wounded from the sophisticated barbs sent my way by the very people who had invited me. Pierre was unfailingly polite and friendly and just raved about my dress, a stunning outfit which was yoked at the top and fell sheer to the waist. When I told him I had borrowed it from the costumes for *Death in Venice*, he congratulated me on finding such an inventive way to avoid choosing one couturier over another.

Shored up by such kindness, I had a thoroughly wonderful meal at Maxim's and partied all night. The guest I remember most vividly is Lauren Bacall. She came right up to me and asked: "How are Justin, Sacha and Micha?"

I was astounded. "How on earth do you know my boys?" I demanded.

Her answer has stayed with me ever since: "I've followed your adventures. You're very brave and I wish you the very best. You simply must hang on to your little boys."

I thought of those words the next day as, still queasy from the ravages of the night before, I posed in the Bois de Boulogne for the cover photo for *Beyond Reason*. Ruefully, I mulled over the chaos of my life. Paris was marvellous, just as London had been, and most of the people I spent my time with were exceptionally creative. It was fun.

If it hadn't worked, that was because I was incomplete. Had I been an integrated person, I could have handled it. As it was, I was torn, hurt and schizophrenic, split between my work and my husband, between my children and myself, spread too thin and inside myself unfinished, searching for something to complete me. I felt very tired. I packed my bags and left for New York – on Concorde, of course.

Chapter Three
Getting Out of Focus

All my life I have believed in the importance of women working. I grew up in a family where work was not just respected but essential – as Minister of Fisheries in the Louis St Laurent government, my father put in long and exhausting hours at his office in Ottawa, and even longer ones at home in Vancouver – and as one of five girls there was never any question that, once I graduated from university, I would find a career of some kind. Even while still at high school I was asked to train as a possible manager for the local Hudson's Bay department store. I turned down the offer, studying political science, sociology and anthropology at Vancouver's Simon Fraser University instead. Before marrying Pierre, I worked as a sociologist in the civil service in Ottawa. It was hideously dull; but it was a job.

Married to Pierre, however, I soon found an immense confusion over the whole question of work. He and I had totally different ideas about what that – when it came to me – actually meant. He assumed that it would be enough for me to be the wife of the Prime Minister and that I had quite enough to do raising sons and being there for him. Because he's very careful not to sound like a chauvinist, he wouldn't say, "I don't want you to work," but he was adamant that there was no question of me returning to school for a master's degree in child psychology at the University of Ottawa, as I had hoped. He used to say, "Married women who go back to university are bored women looking for young men." On this matter Pierre was both possessive and jealous. "Margaret," he said to me one day when I was complaining about my enforced seclusion, "you had a good education. You know how to read and study. Take the classics, the Russians and the Greeks, take your psychology textbooks, and go and read them. After all, we don't *need* the money from you working."

In the beginning, in any case, I too believed that I had a real job to do at 24 Sussex Drive. In fact I had embarked on our entire marriage with the idea of such work firmly in my mind, dreaming happily in the months I prepared for it of how I would become the most polished and charming hostess in Canada, how I would be an asset to Pierre in his political life, how I would learn to manage and direct a fine family home.

At the start of our marriage I was also inundated with requests to represent an enormous number of charities, the only work deemed suitable for a Prime Minister's wife. Some of these I turned down, on the grounds that I did not have the time and that I was not prepared to be a mere figurehead. I did however agree to do TV commercials for the Canadian Mental Health Association and I became honorary chairperson of the national chapter of UNICEF. Later, I wished I had done more charity work, but at that time I was deeply put off by the way people's behaviour altered, becoming stilted and nervous, when Mrs Trudeau, the Prime Minister's wife, stepped out of the car.

Soon, though, my household chores and the charities I spoke for did not fill enough of my life. I grew bored. My dreams about creating a perfect home had been eroded by a combination of a growing loathing for officialdom and the fact that the staff was so efficient that I was no longer needed. The house decorated, the menus sorted out, the boys' routines established – what was there left for me to do?

Pierre and I took to arguing about my work. I begged him to let me go back to my studies. I felt I needed a specialized education, to allow me to work with people, not concepts, and that once I had trained I would easily be able to fit a part-time job into my routine at 24 Sussex. Pierre refused. He is an old-fashioned man when it comes to the position of women in the home, and he wanted me dependent on him.

He is also extremely persuasive, and he soon flattered me into submission by telling me how lucky I was, how needed I was at home, how well loved I was, and how hard I would surely find the strain of doing both. Foolishly, I listened. Being basically lazy by nature, I wasn't really drawn to a nine-to-five job, so I capitulated and spent my time idling away the hours on the terrace looking out at the Rideau River and dreaming.

And after the first few years I found a partial solution to Pierre's possessiveness and my restless desire to pursue a career of my own. In 1974, King Hussein and Queen Alia of Jordan, knowing me to be unhapppy, presented me with a magnificent set of cameras. With these, I set about learning photography. First I studied commercial photography under well-known Canadian photographer Sherman Hines. Next I took lessons from a UPI photographer friend, Rod McIvor, learning darkroom techniques in the news service's Ottawa offices and following photographers around on stories, though Pierre objected strongly to me hanging around with the press. Then I took a course in technical photography at Ottawa's Algonquin Community College. I enjoyed those days vastly. They made me forget who I was.

Not surprisingly, given that it was just about the only

professional training of any kind that I had received, photography was my first choice when looking for work. John Dominis, the picture editor of *People* magazine, unexpectedly came to my aid early in 1977. I admire John very much: he's a magnificent photographer of wild life in Africa and he always manages to look rather like a white hunter off on a safari. When he gave me my interview he was also very tough, very clear about work standards, making it perfectly plain that, if I was going to work for him, the pictures I took were going to have to be professional. I was delighted. This was the very attitude I was looking for. No concessions, but a real job.

Unfortunately, I hadn't reckoned with the gossip side of *People* magazine. The editors soon heard about my assignments and sent reporters to follow me around and write about me while I was working.

During 1977, I completed three photostories for *People*. I did my best work when John sent me to Philadelphia to cover the romantic white hope of the boxing world, Duane Bobick, in his fight against Ken Norton. What no one had realized was that the fight was really nothing more than a media event – the film *Rocky* was just out. Bobick's preoccupation was not with getting up at dawn for early-morning jogging sessions through Philadelphia markets but with what to do with his earnings. I was ready and eager outside his house at 5 am on the day of the fight, but he had been up late the night before with his accountant. I just about missed the great fight altogether: Bobick was downed by Norton in the first minute, lasting just long enough to earn his chunk of the take.

Still, I took the pictures, and they turned out well. To my delight, John praised them technically and gave them a good spread. "Photos by Margaret Trudeau" said the credits, and that was all. My first real job as a skinny little photographer on *People* augured well.

The other two foundered. One, on Bruce Nevins' Perrier water empire, was a loser from the start, and a photostory I went to do on New York's Greenwich Village turned out, when it reached the magazine, to be no more than a vehicle for yet another mean, gossipy article about me.

That was the end of *People* and me. I realized that I was simply not ruthless enough to become one of the paparazzi and go after every sensational story, which seemed to be the only way to make money. The personal cost of doing so – incessant, hateful publicity – was quite simply too high a price to pay.

All through the early summer of 1977, I had been waiting around for a promised tryout on the *Good Morning America* television show. One of the producers, Woody Fraser, held out the possibility of a job as host – but even I realized that at that time I was hardly a respectable representative of clean-living middleclass America. Finally, however, what amounted to a public audition was offered to me. I was to talk about my photography and show my pictures.

It didn't turn out quite that way. The girl who questioned me was snide and hostile and far more interested in Pierre than my darkroom techniques. *People* magazine, the *Good Morning America* show – all they wanted was the photographer, not the photographs. How was I ever going to escape this feeling of being used as the wife of the Prime Minister? How was I going to get *out* of focus?

Those first two work experiences sickened me, but they also made me realize just how much I liked star status and how essential it was for me to achieve it, not as a wife, but in my own right. So I turned to acting. I joined a very tough advanced course run by Wynn Handman in New York and learned two crucial lessons: that to become a good actress you have to work very hard indeed, and that it was quite impossible for me to behave as if I was a poor starving drama student when I had three children and a mansion to run in Ottawa.

Still, that acting experience, combined with my appearance on the *Good Morning America* show, brought me my first film part. It was December 1977. A Canadian director called Alexis Kanner got in touch to ask whether I would like to co-star with Patrick McGoohan in a film called *Kings and Desperate Men*. He offered me thirty thousand dollars. It seemed unbelievable.

Even the plot was appealing. I was to be Elizabeth Kingsley, the wife of a failed actor who was now a controversial radio talk-show host. I was to be kidnapped with my son, husband and a federal judge by a gang of intellectual terrorists. A lovely, protected, rich little girl who grows up through a long night of terror and comes to see that the man she married is no more than an empty, crude womanizer, a cheat and a liar.

That turned out to be the problem. I threw myself into the part – too well. I wasn't helped by the natural animosity between myself and Patrick McGoohan that was obvious even before we started work together. I had never met Patrick before, though I had long admired his intensely blue eyes and his skills as an actor. Alexis introduced us on the set, which had been built on the top floor of Montreal's Four Seasons Hotel, where we were also staying. I was surprised to see a distinctly frightened look in his eyes: perhaps he was shy, certainly he gave the impression of mistrusting me profoundly. We didn't say much on that occasion, so our first real encounter was later in the day, and it was a far from pleasant one.

On my arrival in Montreal to start shooting, I had been offered the best suite in the hotel: I had turned it down, principally because the idea of living alone in such enormous splendour appalled me. Patrick McGoohan chose to see in my preference for a smaller room down the corridor a mockery of *his* enormous suite and as I was walking past his door said, nastily: "What are *you* doing here?"

"I'm going to my room," I replied, as pleasantly as possible.

He spluttered with scorn. Patrick McGoohan is not the sort of man I like: perfect for his part, but far too like it in life to be agreeable, a big surly man with an awful temper.

Sensing my own temper rise, I stopped. "Mr McGoohan, I'm very new at making movies and I want to do it properly, so may I ask you one question?"

He simpered immediately, placated by all this buttering up.

"It must be very important for an actor and actress to respect each other?"

He nodded.

I went on. "I do respect you as a professional, but now tell me something: Do I have to like you? I mean, is that important?"

He began to look uncomfortable, shook his head.

"Good. Because, Mr McGoohan, I do not like you, and I don't see that changing."

It wasn't a good start. I soon regretted my hasty temper as the media clamoured around me while McGoohan got brushed aside. As he became more frustrated he took it upon himself to cut my lines. Every time I had a big scene coming up he would call me over, take out a fat black pencil and, putting out his hand for my script, start removing lines.

I soon sensed that both he and the director were really playing a game with me in order to get me into the right mood for the script. I was supposed to be a terrified, confused and hurt woman – and, by the time Patrick McGoohan had finished with me, I certainly was. I kept remembering Candice Bergen talking about a film she made with Lina Wertmuller and Giancarlo Giannini in which they set her up and played with her, like cat and mouse, in order to trap her into an excellent performance. I knew it was done all the time, but I found it insulting. I kept telling them: "You don't have to make me cry, I can cry. I can find it within myself to do it."

Our final bustup came, fortunately, on Christmas Eve of 1977 at the very end of the shooting. We were to have a beautiful reconciliation scene with a happy ending in which I was also to voice my despair over what had happened. The trouble was, I was by now far too deeply into my part to believe it possible that I could ever become reconciled to this drunken womanizer and besides that, Patrick McGoohan was hell bent on giving me nothing to say.

The day started badly. He managed to drop all my lines except for the word "fine." But having scored out the rest he hadn't written down the one word. We started filming. The moment came for me to say "fine." Nothing happened. He hurtled over.

"What's going on?"

"Nothing," I replied. "You've cut my lines."

"But what about 'fine'?"

"It's not *fine*," I replied in fury.

We took our quarrel off the set. By now McGoohan was storming around, shouting that he would get me fired unless I did what he said. "We can replace you this instant," he said. "We'll shoot any girl in what you're wearing, from the side. There must be ten girls walking down Sherbrooke Street at this moment who could step in here and do what you're doing – far better than you're doing it."

I had one more card to play.

"Mr McGoohan, you can't begin to know how happy I would be if I could walk off this set right now and never set eyes on you again. But if I leave this set this raincoat goes with me, because most of the wardrobe is mine, and I can promise you that you'll have a hard time matching it on Christmas Eve in Canada."

He gave me no more trouble.

After their initial skepticism, the members of the crew had warmed to me, as they saw I really was doing my utmost to learn to play my part. I spent a great deal of time with them listening to the technicalities of filmmaking. I also learned a lot from Alexis, though I found him a bit of a megalomaniac in the way he saw himself as Orson Welles – leading man, supporting actor, writer and editor. He couldn't delegate and became ever more possessive about the film, and in the end it took three years before he deemed it ready for release. It finally premiered in Montreal in August 1981.

My real friend and inspiration was my co-leading lady, an American actress called Andrea Marcovicci who took her art seriously and went to great lengths to teach me. We also shared a sense of exasperation over Patrick McGoohan who, she said, was the hardest man she had ever had to work with.

I had learned a lot from *Kings and Desperate Men*: I had discovered that I loved the life, I loved the camaraderie with the crew, the teamwork, and most of all I loved the fantasy world of acting, the way that I could let out all the emotions I usually had to keep in check. And so I pondered, as I cast about over the next months, reflecting on my future. The previous summer my romance with Jack Nicholson had concluded with brutal finality. It was becoming clear to me from my seedy months around New York and London that there was to be no salvation through people. Perhaps it lay with work?

Once again, I was saved by an invitation. Some French and Canadian producers were planning to make a co-production in the south of France about Annie, the mistress of a wealthy Canadian businessman who comes to

France on holiday and has a series of light flirtations with three very different men only to find that her lover has had her followed by a private detective. It was to be called *L'Ange Guardien* (*The Guardian Angel*). Jean-Luc Terrade was to play my yoga suitor, Jean-Luc Fritz the beachboy and Michel Louvain my pianist lover. The leading man, the detective Aldo who later falls in love with the woman he is following, was to be Francis Lemaire. Would I, for fifty thousand dollars, play the part of Annie?

It was the spring of 1978. I needed the money, I wanted work, here was the solution to my life. I packed the clothes I had bought so wildly in London and made my way as fast as I could to Cassis, to a charming hotel called Les Jardins overlooking the Mediterranean. From the balcony of my cottage suite I could sit in the evenings and watch the cliffs turn from pale pink to spectacular deep raspberry red in the setting sun.

It was soon apparent, however, that this was no team of professionals. The script had been written by a gynecologist; I only hope that he was better at his gynecology than he was at writing. I wondered about Jacques Fournier's ability to direct; the French film company had never made a feature movie. Only the members of the Canadian team were old hands, and they were appalled to find out what a Mickey Mouse setup it all was.

From the first, there was chaos. Fournier, thinking that the best way to show a busy resort in summer was to stuff every scene with twenty extras too many, so fussed up the settings that it was impossible to tell what was going on. The rushes looked dreadful. Then he had no idea about camera angles or booms or lighting or how to get close to a subject. The scene in which I was pursued by the yogi showed two ant-like figures from an immense distance scurrying about across a mountain-

53

side (rather like an early Charlie Chaplin movie) and ended with me hurling myself off one of the cliffs that make the region so splendid, ostensibly into water. In fact, as was only too plain to all viewers, I landed on a mattress laid out just over the edge.

Then came the scene in which I was to be sunbathing and awaken to find myself under assault by the man with whom I was spending the day. That would have been fine, only Fournier directed me to lie down on a rocky road, with no towel underneath and great boulders sticking up. What would I, supposedly this glamorous sexy woman on holiday, be doing prone on a lot of rocks? (Later a Canadian television programme, *W5*, called a story it featured about me on location *Margaret's Rocky Road*.)

But there were comic moments. One of my heart-throbs was not, in real life, a ladies' man. It fell to him to have to rape me in a cloakroom. We got ourselves arranged, but the second before the director called "action," my rapist hastily reached for his handbag, took out a can of Binaca clean breath spray, gave his mouth a bit of a squirt, reached up again, and took out some after-shave cologne – all this so that I would not be offended by the smell of his body. I laughed so much they had to hold the shooting.

There were also good times. Cassis is one of the prettier resorts in the south of France, its terra cotta and shuttered port protected by planning laws and its narrow streets, unchanged since Scott Fitzgerald's days, largely closed to cars. I ate marvellous seafood in the little restaurants overlooking the fishing boats, swam in the translucent aquamarine waters of the Calanques, the little rocky inlets where submarines used to surface to unload provisions for the Maquis during the Second World War.

One weekend I was given a few days off and went

down to Monte Carlo to stay with my friend Régine who was opening her own club there. It was wonderful, a far cry from the sleaziness of the film unit. After all the catastrophes, the hours of waiting around, the early calls and general incompetence, I was charmed by the sophistication and elegance of her club, Jimmy's. It was a marvel of excellent food and good lighting. I spent my time talking to tennis star Bjorn Borg and eating caviar and wondering if I preferred this sort of club – for the rich and the jet-setters but infinitely respectable – to the arty freakiness of places like Studio 54.

One of the troubles on the set was a pervasive sexual jealousy. The director was furious when I became involved with the charming, incredibly handsome but penniless Jean-Luc Fritz, who played the part of the beachboy. Jean-Luc did his best to protect me from the tackiness of the film life.

Soon, too, I began to feel exploited. All my horror and hatred of being used, being indulged and touted around not for what I could do but for who I was, began to surface. It wouldn't have taken Einstein to realize that I was in Cassis, not because of my talents as an actress, but because it was a neat scheme to make a film about Margaret Trudeau, wife of the Prime Minister of Canada, well-known jet-setter, running about with a lot of men in the south of France.

From the day I got there reporters had flown in from all over the world. Had I left my husband? What about my children? What did I think of Frenchmen? I refused to give interviews about my private life, but that didn't seem to protect me, and I soon became more obsessed and miserable than ever, doubting myself as an actress, guilty about my boys so far away. What the reporters couldn't get, they made up. And the film company was not disposed to help. After all, this was wonderful publicity for them. I kept saying: "Why have you hired me?

As an actress, or a publicity stunt?" Fournier, by then angry with me over Jean-Luc, merely shrugged.

When the day arrived for me to leave, there was still no ticket. The last few days had been a nightmare: the Canadian crew, infuriated with the incompetence and no longer being paid since the production had run out of money, had walked out, leaving a bunch of truly hopeless amateurs to try and patch together an ending. The producer assured me my ticket was waiting at the airport. I booked a flight, took the little local train that winds through the scrub and umbrella pine forest, and finally reached Marseilles airport. No ticket. I phoned the company office: no one there. It dawned on me then that there wasn't going to be a ticket. It was this final stroke of meanness that gave me the ammunition to decline all publicity and promotional work for the film, so that when it premiered in Montreal in December of 1978, I was not there to lend a hand.

My acting career might well have been ended forever after this experience had it not been for an unexpected and welcome encounter. I got home to Ottawa to find an excited message from my close friend Nancy Pitfield, the wife of Pierre's cabinet secretary, Michael Pitfield. "Come on over at once," it said. "I've got something incredible to tell you."

When I got to her house she rushed to the door. "Guess who's looking for you?"

I laughed: "Warren Beatty?"

Her face fell: "How *did* you know?"

I didn't, of course; it was just an inspired guess. Nancy told me how she had been cooking dinner and trying to get her three children into bed one night when the phone rang and a strange voice said: "Please excuse me for bothering you, but I understand that you're a friend of Margaret Trudeau and I want to get a message to her."

"Who are you?" she asked.

"Warren Beatty," the pleasant-sounding stranger replied.

To which she smartly retorted: "Oh sure."

The message was merely to call him. When I got through, he said he needed to talk to me and asked whether I was ever in New York. I wasn't planning a trip but was pleased for the excuse, and deeply curious anyway, so we arranged to meet for drinks in the bar of the Carlyle Hotel. I am always optimistic. Until something happens to disprove it, I always think that something wonderful is about to happen.

From the minute I saw him I felt easy in his company. He was an intelligent, funny, charming man. While he had nothing concrete to offer, he told me he arranged the meeting to discuss future movie possibilities and to tell me that he thought I had every chance of becoming a great actress for one very simple reason: my tremendous inner rage, vital for a good actress. "No one makes a good actor," he said, "unless he has a whole fund of emotions inside him, real emotions which have not been studied and about which you don't have to pretend but simply draw upon when you need them for a part."

His extreme friendliness relaxed me. I told him about the domineering behaviour of McGoohan in *Kings and Desperate Men*, about the amateur chaos of *L'Ange Guardien*, about how I felt exploited with no sense of myself as an actress. He reassured me. He told me to work hard, study drama more seriously. He said I probably would not make a really good actress until I had worked out the life I was leading. Then, and only then, should I look for more film work.

"Oh no," I told him, "this was my last film. It was just a complete turkey."

He laughed. "We all make turkeys, Margaret. That's the way we grow in our profession."

At that time, the love of Warren Beatty's life was Diane

Keaton. I don't know whether it was her watching technique that was keeping him so very faithful, but I do know that she had him paged three times during the three hours we were having drinks, just to be sure we hadn't retired to his suite, which I later reflected would not have been such a hardship.

As it was, all he offered to do was to walk me back to my friend's apartment on Park Avenue. While we were strolling slowly along, I told him the story of my disastrous adventure with Jack Nicholson.

"Jack's a terrible masochist," was all he said when I finished. "The only thing that would have made him happy would have been if you had sat on his face and shat on it." We both laughed and I felt comforted.

Indeed, the whole encounter made me feel good. For one thing, it had been entirely professional; no seduction involved. For another, Warren managed to instill in me a feeling of self-respect. I had no illusions that I would be the next Warren Beatty leading lady, but I did reflect that if he could see some possible talent in me, then why not have hope?

Chapter Four
Mrs Rochester at 24 Sussex Drive

This talk of the high life I was leading could easily give
the impression that I had totally abandoned Pierre and
the children. It was a picture generously fuelled by the
press, which fed the public a constant meal of rumours.
Some said that Pierre had given me a million dollars to
get me out of his life; others that I spent my nights
camping out in Studio 54; others again that I was still no
more than a flower child and had reverted to my hippie
ways. I was a Nathaniel Hawthorne character, with a
scarlet A emblazoned on my bosom.

The truth was very different. In the spring of 1977 I
had indeed forsaken the life led by the Prime Minister's
wife, with its official functions and its highly vaunted
privileges, not because I was no good at it, not because I
hated it (who could really hate being pampered the way I
was?), but because I needed money and because my
relationship with Pierre was going very wrong. I had
not, until November 1979, completely parted from him,
for we thought constantly about reconciliation, and I had
certainly not abandoned my children. That's what made
the rumours so very cruel: how could I have abandoned
my children? The very notion was so unreal to me that it
hadn't occurred to me that it might be seen that way.

Even had I wanted to leave home, I would not have

been able to do so: I had no money of my own, no way of offering a home to my three sons and I was in any case far from confident in myself. So Pierre and I had evolved a curious and highly secretive way of life. Every two or three weeks I would disappear to New York or London. Then, after ten days or two weeks, I would become so homesick, so desperate to get back to the boys, that I would return to Canada.

It was then, during those first few days after each return, that I would find it hard to resist Pierre and his dreams. We lived, I sometimes thought, on a diet of dreams. Pierre, seeing my uncertainty, would ply me with plans about our future, the house we would build when he left politics, the ponies we would have for the children, the Japanese room he would build me for my special cooking. I would bask gloriously in the anticipation of such happiness. Then the dreams would pale, all our incompatibilities would come flooding back and I would flee Ottawa again in search of a world that seemed to understand me better. And so on, the same routine, month after month.

Meanwhile, I had made one basic decision. I moved out of the splendid master bedroom on the second floor, with its view over the Rideau River toward Quebec, its bright yellow Thai silk wallpaper, huge brass bed and embroidered Madeira linen sheets, its famed collection of Canadiana furniture inherited from Maryon Pearson, wife of former Prime Minister Lester Pearson, and up to the third floor, to what used to be my sewing room, a sunny, charming, sloping attic room with a view over the garden. Next door was a little spare guest room and bathroom, papered in a striped sprig flower design, and furnished with a birdseed maple double bed, armoire and dressing table which had once been part of Pierre's mother's trousseau. These three rooms I now made my own. I was not altogether sad to have the intimacy of my attic in exchange for the formal and cold grandeur of the grey stone mansion with its official rooms that no amount of redecoration had really begun to cheer.

Up there, overnight, I became poor mad Mrs Rochester in *Jane Eyre*, the distant spectator, the hidden wife. By mutual decision Pierre told no one of my plans, simply refusing to speak of them, and he is not the sort of man one questions easily. Justin (by now six), Sacha (four), and Micha (two) watched my moves – but, being so young, accepted them. When I was away, I was "Mummy working hard at a career as film actress." When I was home I had simply changed one bedroom for another. Since Pierre had a dressing room of his own off the master bedroom, they accepted the fact that we always used two rooms. Pierre's political colleagues knew nothing more than what they read in the papers.

To govern our new life, however, Pierre laid down a few rules. He was perfectly prepared to be supportive while I looked for work and decided about my future, but he would not give me money and he would not contemplate me taking the children away from him. I was perfectly free to come and go, but they were to stay with him.

I wouldn't have dreamed of fighting him over either of these demands. Even during an earlier trial separation Pierre had refused to pay any of my bills and by now I had become proud – perhaps, with hindsight, intimidated – about asking for help. "I don't *need* your money," I used to say, furiously, whenever he felt bound to say once again that he was not giving me any. "How *dare* you think that I'm after it?" As for the children, it never crossed my mind to try and take them from him. I still loved Pierre, even if only in a sad way, and I wouldn't have hurt him that way. Besides, I needed to go on my own.

To the two main rules Pierre added two more: no

interference in his life; no scandals or embarrassments of any kind. Strange as it may now sound, this was fine by me. Since I was away so much all I wanted to do when in Ottawa was to be the best mother I could. I had no other life there anyway, so while at 24 Sussex I wanted to give myself up to the boys. I didn't want another life: I was growing up, becoming at last a person on my own, and painful as I found them, the restraints helped.

In this, Pierre helped me, and as I grew and changed, so our relationship changed. There had always been an underlying current between us over and above that of a husband and a wife: that of a father and daughter. Now, when I returned to Ottawa full of good jokes and funny stories, bolstered by the affection and approval of my new friends, forgetting the anxiety I so often felt when I was with them, I regaled Pierre with tales of my adventures. He seemed to delight in hearing me talk and I soon felt that I was reporting back to him. I needed Pierre, and I needed to be there myself in order to keep him informed about how I was growing up. And so gradually our attitudes toward one another altered. Pierre became ever more paternal, as I was increasingly the eldest of his children, just leaving the nest. He seemed to love me to be as young as I could be.

On the domestic side, there were really very few problems. The highly efficient staff of 24 Sussex consisted of some ten people who between them had the house in excellent order (in *too* good order perhaps, for I never could bear that excessive tidiness that comes from having many servants, that absolute absence of all homely clutter, which made its mark so strongly that the last thing I did before leaving on each of my trips was to tidy every single one of my possessions out of sight).

Most of the people I had employed were still there. There was Hildegard, the senior maid, a kindly woman who did her best to smooth my path; Ruth, the staff and children's cook, a loving, decent woman; and Yannick Vincent, the burly French chef who raised sled dogs in his spare time and used to leave meals for me when he knew my plane was arriving late. Nobody seemed to mind that my involvement in the menus and the food became increasingly sporadic, for I quickly discovered in myself an extraordinary reluctance, on getting home, to sit down every Monday morning and decide every dish from soup to dessert for an entire week. Or, if they minded, they took care not to let me see, for I found them wonderfully supportive, eager, on my return, to cater to my every whim, to make me feel welcome. They treated me like the undisputed mistress of the household. Mary Alice, the ex-nun who was the housekeeper, even put off having her baby in order to be there for me to turn to. They seemed to care genuinely about Pierre and me and were still hoping things would work out between us.

Just the same, I sometimes felt as if I were regressing into childhood again. A lot of this came from my guilt. I could not bear to think that I was letting down all those Canadian people who had sent me presents on our sons' birthdays and shown up to cheer us at official gatherings, people who had seen in us a model family. Since I was behaving in a way that can only be described as bad I came to feel that I did not deserve the pampering that went with my official life. So I tried to deny myself the pleasures of being served and waited on, and apart from the laundry tried to do as much as possible for myself. This only led to greater muddle.

Within days of my return it was as if I had never been away. Yet at the same time I remained a stranger in the sense that I was really only there for the children. I came to regard myself as an extra nanny, someone brought in to help with the children. I wasn't even an ordinary visitor, because I turned down all the services that visitors get. And yet at the same time Pierre and I had a lot to work out together, and he hated me to use 24 Sussex only as a place to stay. When at home he wanted me properly at home, eating with him, sharing his life, and he resented it bitterly if I went out to spend an evening with a girlfriend. I became increasingly confused, for there were nights when I wanted to cry on his shoulder.

My growing uncertainty about my identity was later aggravated by one of the few newcomers to the team, Heidi Bennett, a German housekeeper with two daughters of her own. She had been brought in to preside over the house in the spring of 1978 after Mary Alice had finally left to begin her family. From the first I found her chilly, ambitious and keenly resentful of me; she must have found me tiresome and interfering. But our relations grew rapidly worse as she began to assume roles that had been mine. From merely supervising the household, she took to greeting Pierre's dinner guests – whether I was away, or upstairs, listening down the stairwell – decked out in a chiffon dress, acting as hostess and making sure they had the drinks they liked. She irked me too by the way she had set herself up as a guru on separation. She was divorced herself, and always ready to interject little bits of advice.

The children, meanwhile, were in the hands of two nannies. There was Monica Mallon, a university-educated girl, one of eight children, who had worked in children's hospitals and had taken over the care of Michel, the baby, when he outgrew Tara Virgo, my Jamaican maid. And there was Vicky Kimberley, a pretty, seemingly cold blonde of twenty-one who was in fact highly conscientious about doing constructive things with the older boys, both of whom adored her. While I was away, there was always at least one of them in residence.

Sometimes I felt the boys were now in such good hands that I had to restrain myself from becoming too involved when I was there, fearing to upset the measured routine of their days. But the nannies, Monica in particular, went to great lengths to dispel this feeling, making no moves themselves to take the boys over and emphasizing how very much they needed me. To compensate for my absences I came home bearing wonderful gifts, so my homecomings were always moments of great rejoicing, and I would make up for my absences with two very loving weeks.

On a practical level, what I did was spell the nannies, so that once I got home I took the children out for treats to McDonald's or to visit friends with boys their age. I also ate lunch with them, down in their playroom, having moved them from the staff dining room because I felt that it was too full of older women telling them how to behave. And I supervised their suppers. Michel and Justin loved Ruth's Jell-o desserts. Sacha yearned for Yannick's smoked salmon and escargots.

Those of Pierre's immediate political staff, who could hardly fail to see what was going on, were unfailingly polite and helpful, but I soon came to see that it was very unfair of me to try and have close relationships with any of them. It only asked them to divide their loyalty.

Joyce Fairburn, Pierre's legislative assistant who handles his liaison with Parliament, provides a good example. Joyce and her husband Michael Gillan were very good friends and I used to spend a lot of time over at their house, talking about what was happening to Pierre and me. But Joyce's job was, after all, to keep Pierre informed about everything that went on, and I was disturbed to realize that she thought it her duty to report *everything*. It was inevitable, and I should not have put that sort of strain on her.

Then there were the Pitfields, both good and old friends of ours. I talked a lot to Nancy, and that didn't matter so much because she was one of my oldest

65

friends. But I knew I was being too demanding when I tried to get Michael, Pierre's cabinet secretary and a loving, gentle man, to intercede with Pierre on my behalf. Other than these friends, it wasn't hard to stay detached: I had never seen very much of Pierre's staff.

At the same time I could never quite escape the snide and hurtful episodes, even if they sometimes came from people who intended no harm. I went to some lengths never to read anything written about me in papers or listen to gossip, so that was some kind of protection. But I could not avoid the smaller, more hurtful cracks, and these invariably reduced me to tears. There was the time when I came home to be greeted by one of the children's RCMP security men, a man too familiar in manner who overstepped his bounds and saw himself as a match-maker. He wanted to make me feel guilty and bring me back home again. So he came up to me and said: "Oh, Mrs Trudeau, I'm so glad you're back. The little boys sure do miss you while you're away. You can really tell it when you see them . . . the way they behave when you're not here . . ." and so on. I knew he was wrong, but how could it not make me feel guilty?

More frightening, though as it turned out, unimportant, was the story of Michel's tonsils. It gave both Pierre and me a severe scare. On one occasion, returning home from New York, I was met at Ottawa airport by the official limousine with Monica and the three boys inside. Michel, I noticed immediately, had yet another bad cold. I knew he had been for a checkup so I asked Monica what the doctor had said about his tonsils.

"Surely it's time they came out. They're like golf balls."

"Oh," she replied casually, "Michel can't have his tonsils out until he is five or six because of the hole in his heart."

"The *what* in his *what*?" I was seized with panic.

She looked surprised. "Well, he has this lesion in his heart."

I wasn't sure whether I was more furious or worried. I tried to keep calm. "That's news to me Monica. How long have you known that?"

She thought for a minute. "Well I guess Dr McKee told me last time I took the children to see him for a checkup. Nine or ten months ago."

"Did you tell my husband?"

Monica began to look uncomfortable. "Er, no, I thought you both knew."

This was pure agony. There might have been something seriously wrong with Micha, still not much more than a baby, and I, his mother, had no clue about it.

When I told Pierre, he also shook with rage: how did all these people presume to keep from us, Michel's parents, news of such importance? Actually the lesion turned out to be far from serious and Dr Jim McKee, when I reached him, assured me that many children have a minor imperfection of this kind. The event also provided us with a shock that possibly we needed: smoothly as the system functioned at 24 Sussex, it was still not smoothly enough.

Publicly, my situation was always peculiar. However firmly I had rejected my stuffed-shirt role as wife to the Prime Minister, unruffled hostess to bores and charmers alike, however passionately I now believed that the position of political wife is not a tenable one with its humiliating assumptions of subservience, I still found it very strange to be in a house where it all went on without me. Pierre had been adamant on this point: a crucial part of the bargain was that no one should know of my comings and goings.

People like Michael Pitfield and Jim Coutts, then Pierre's chief of staff, knew I was there, of course, and so did his exemplary secretary Miss Cecile Viau, a devoted aide of many years who knew better than anyone what was happening and kept it all to herself. Others who passed through the house for official meetings had to conceal their astonishment when they bumped into me supervising a flower arrangement, discussing food with the chef or talking to Mrs Bennett about some forthcoming official function. If it sounds strange that I was doing these things at all, it was simply that I fell back into them naturally and I had nothing else to do. I still felt an immense pride in the house, in how fine I had made it look – perhaps the only thing I did feel pride in – and I took pleasure in keeping it all up to scratch.

For all other occasions, however informal, I was expected to keep to my quarters. I would switch my lights off and perch on the window seats of my attic sitting room listening to the voices of the guests as they arrived, and later watch them in their black ties and long dresses, their jewellery sparkling, as they strolled in the garden after dinner, with the lights from the shores of the river beyond them. I remembered the many evenings I had strolled there myself, the many formal occasions I had organized and enjoyed at 24 Sussex, particularly the evening the Queen came to dinner, my first real guest at the redecorated and redesigned Prime Minister's home. Those nights, I felt very lonely indeed.

I felt used, too. However well the staff now ran 24 Sussex, I still felt it needed a touch none of them seemed to be able to provide, a feeling of elegance that I had always prided myself on. So when any formal occasion was planned I still felt it to be my somewhat sad duty to select the flowers from the greenhouse I had set up, to spend time with Yannick working out a menu, to make sure the table had been set to perfection.

When Pierre was receiving old mutual friends I was not just allowed down but actively welcomed among them. It did not happen often, but they were certainly the best evenings we had together. They made me forget what was happening to us by taking some of the pressure off. Pierre and I could look at each other, and admire each other, but at a distance. And I loved all the good stories and jokes. It was good having a little bit of fun in the midst of all the trouble.

One day Lady Mary Mitchell came to Ottawa with her husband, Sir Harold Mitchell, a Tory MP in the British government. It was at Frankfort, Lady Mary's splendid Jamaican guest villa with its breathtaking gardens (since it was Lady Mary's wish that she would never see an inch of bare earth their property was a profusion of flowers and bushes, orchids and jade trees) that Pierre and I had spent many, and often sadly quarrelsome, holidays during our married life. We had a pleasant dinner, but in the bedroom afterward I told Mary what was happening to us. She is in her late sixties, a worldly, intelligent, humorous woman, the one of my friends most like a mother to me. She was not surprised to find things the way they were. "You're too far apart in age," she told me now. "Pierre is quite simply too old for you."

Another time Charles Bedard, an old friend of Pierre, came with his wife, Jacinthe, to dinner, and I joined the party. On occasion, too, if Pierre was having a very small dinner for people passing through Ottawa who interested him, people such as author Alvin Toffler or violinist Yehudi Menuhin, he would ask me to take part. These were people who knew nothing about us and had no dealings with Canadian life. If they were surprised to find me there they were far too polite to show it.

This role took new shape when in the winter of 1979 Mr and Mrs Jules Léger, the retiring Governor General and his wife, were to attend a farewell dinner for 250 people hosted by Pierre. They had served their term for five years, and the government was honouring them with a reception for Canada's foremost politicians, businessmen and diplomats. This came at the end of one of my longest unbroken stays at 24 Sussex and I was feeling once again very much a part of the household. Pierre had not, of course, suggested that I accompany him, but had asked me instead to act as hostess for a cocktail party he was to give for members of his family and close friends who had come from Montreal for the reception.

I threw myself with goodwill into organizing our guests' bedrooms and arranging their meals. At nine o'clock on the night of the ball the last guests left for the gala event. I heard their laughter in the driveway, the banging of car doors. I turned back into the hall and climbed the stairs to my attic rooms. That was a bitter taste indeed.

Chapter Five
Private Lives

Privately, Pierre and I were living curious lives. During the spells when I was at home from spring 1977 until autumn 1979, the routine of our days was much as it had always been, apart from my attic seclusion and the way in which I was barred from official life. But since Pierre is not by nature very gregarious we had always spent a great deal of time alone with the children, and this we continued to do although horribly distanced from each other. In appearance, in fact, our lives sometimes assumed so much the taste and shape of our happy past that I could almost fool myself into believing we were in love again.

Family life began at six forty-five each evening. Until then Pierre had gone his official way, working in his office, lunching with colleagues. He dropped in to see the boys only for a few minutes at breakfast and lunch. Meanwhile Justin, Sacha, Michel and I shared a domestic and calm day of school, meals, friends and nursery.

But at six forty-five Pierre would appear and head directly for the indoor pool he had built behind the house early in our marriage (it is connected to the main building by an underground tunnel).

Undress; into the pool; forty-four laps. Never more; never less. And then he was ready for the boys.

I went with them but never swam; like a cat, I hate getting myself wet. But I would crouch by the side and admire Pierre's immense patience as he coaxed the boys through the water, Micha in his "floaties," Justin and Sacha little fish snaking fearlessly up and down the deep end.

Pierre is a man of punctilious exactitude: after fifteen minutes the boys would be bundled out, wet-haired and sleek, into my arms, and we would carry them upstairs to dry their hair and put them into their pyjamas. Since the nannies left after the boys' early supper, Pierre would help me, teasing them, reading to them, listening to their prayers.

These interludes were extraordinarily happy. They were also the times when Pierre and I tried to sort out any confusion in the boys' minds about values and ethics. In all this, Pierre was a splendid teacher. It wasn't just that he spent hours teaching them how to dive, canoe, do karate and judo, or that he took pains over their table manners. He also read to them every Sunday night from the Bible and tried to interest them in the world, in the customs and habits of different countries. Sacha was the great questioner. Every night that Pierre was at home, Sacha would call to him to come and sit on his bed and there he would pester him with questions on every conceivable topic.

We had very little public life as a family. So little, in fact, that when Justin was confirmed at St Brigid's Catholic church and a newspaper photographer caught us kneeling in a row (personally I thought we looked very holy indeed), the editor saw fit to subtitle it "A very rare family outing." The only place we went to outside 24 Sussex was Harrington, the rambling, wooden, two-storey house by the lake, traditionally the country home of Canada's prime ministers but a place I had made very much my own, with vegetable gardens and extremely simple pine furniture. I found these outings dreadfully sad. They brought home to me painfully what had happened to my marriage. Pierre and I had been so very happy at Harrington. In our jeans and beat-up jackets we had canoed and swum, hiked and cooked barbecues. Now my heart was no longer in it.

During the months after our separation Pierre's attitude toward the children was changing. He had always been a doting father, but at a distance. Now the times that I was away were forcing onto him the chores of parenthood, and far from finding them unpleasant or boring Pierre was revelling in them. These two- and three-week stretches of single parenthood were a revelation to him and did much not just to compensate for his feeling of loss in our marriage, but to provide a basic, unbreakable bond with his sons. He became, as I jokingly told him, a very good mother.

Certainly we had difficulties with the children, but they were minor ones and do not seem to have left a mark. Pierre and I were always extremely careful to preserve the notion that we were still a totally united family. When I was at home we tried to do everything together. We never fought in front of them. When I was away Pierre used to talk about me a lot, explaining that I was looking for a career because there was no work for me in Ottawa. I would phone constantly. I think my own childhood, and my mother's strengths and values, helped me to be aware of what problems to look out for.

Sacha was perhaps the most troubled by our divided lives, but then he was born a troubled child, ill at ease even as a baby. His age, four, and the fact that he was the middle son, didn't make it any easier for him. I found, for instance, that after one of my weeks away he would seem delighted to see me, but then explode with rage over seemingly unimportant things. I fretted over these outbursts, but Pierre was wonderful. The angrier and more defiant and aggressive Sacha became, the more love and attention Pierre lavished on him. I think it cemented their love for one another.

Then Justin went through a phase of falling asleep at school. I went to see his teacher who told me that she always knew when I was away because Justin seemed to daydream and doze all the time. After that I made a point of talking a lot more to Justin about what I was doing, so that he felt more involved with me. He soon got over his sleepiness.

Neither Pierre nor I really felt that we had much to worry about. We all – friends, nannies, relatives, the two of us – were watching them closely for bad reactions, and they seemed to us fine. There were so many examples of their sanity and strength to prove it. One day I was driving in the car with the three of them when Sacha suddenly piped up:

"You know, Mummy, I'm famous."

I laughed. "Oh, are you indeed? I didn't know you were famous. You have a famous Daddy, and he's worked very hard to be famous, but I don't think little boys are famous."

Sacha fell silent. But now Justin joined in.

"But Mummy, *you're* famous. *You're* a movie star."

I was touched. He sounded so loving. He continued: "I'm going to be famous too when I grow up. I'm going to be a magician."

Sacha was not to be outdone. "So am I. I'm going to be a famous forest ranger." He paused, troubled by a sudden doubt that forest rangers could be famous. "And while I'm sitting in the tower watching for fires and birds I'll think of a poison to give to people to kill all the sickness in them but not kill them."

I felt he needed praise. "That's good, Sacha. That will be a cure for cancer and will certainly make you famous."

Until then, Micha, the baby, had just listened. But he is

not a child to be left out. He tapped me on the shoulder to get my attention. "Mummy, I'm *not* going to be famous. I'm just going to be an ordinary prime minister."

With conversations like these going on all the time, I didn't feel the boys were suffering.

I was, though. As the months went on, and the newspapers published more stories about my exotic escapades, Pierre grew in public esteem. I came to hate the public goody-goodies who were quick to condemn me, and to praise darling Pierre coping with his three lovely poor little boys. I felt what we were going through was private and that members of the public should be keeping their noses out of our lives instead of becoming ever more vindictive and malicious. It wasn't as if I had abandoned the children in a bungalow in the suburbs and gone off to disco dance every night: Pierre had two nannies, two cooks and five maids – the boys were hardly destitute quite apart from the extraordinary love and attention lavished on them in my absence by one of my friends, Heather Gillin.

Heather is a supermum, there is no other word for it, almost to the point of fanaticism. She is married to a property developer and lives near 24 Sussex. Her eldest son Jeffrey is Justin's best friend; her second son Christopher is also exactly Sacha's age, so the weeks I was away she became a mother to the whole lot of them.

I would be lying if I didn't say that Pierre and I fought when I did come home. Looking back on it, I cannot really remember an evening when, after the boys had gone to bed, we did not hurl abuse at each other. Who is to blame? Who is right? Whose fault is it? Who is wrong? Values and money, those were our main topics of discussion – those and the fact that Pierre refused to accept any blame at all for our problems. "Margaret," he said to me once, "I've never failed at anything. I'm certainly not going to fail at my marriage."

Yannick's fine French food would be ceremoniously presented by a maid on the white, gold and orange Ginori plates I had so lovingly selected, while we bit our lips to stop bickering in front of the servants. The table cleared, we quarrelled, shouted, remembered past insults and episodes and brought them up again and again, while the stern harridan with glasses slipping down her nose – a former joke between Pierre and me – stared down balefully at us from her portrait on the wall.

I knew what I was doing. Venting my rage on Pierre for condemning me to a life I hated and could not handle. Trying to hit out at him because he seemed to be impervious to my attacks. I felt ashamed, but I could not stop. Also, as the months went by, I felt more confused, more scared.

I knew, too, what he was doing. He was punishing me. I think I understood how hurt he was: he couldn't sleep, he looked drawn and sad. But his anguish took the form of attacking me, my morals, my motives, hammering away at me with questions and diatribes. I just wouldn't take the entire blame for our breakdown: I wanted him to understand that it was his fault as well.

Sometime during the autumn of 1977 Pierre started dating. Pierre is a fervent Catholic with rigid moral standards, and I knew beyond any shadow of a doubt that he had been totally faithful to me while we were properly married. But now that we had embarked on our separation I was almost relieved to find that he was prepared to start taking out other women. For one thing I felt that it would make him happier, make him stop longing for me, stop looking so pained when I was around. For another I thought that once he encountered my sort of behaviour in other women it would dispel the notion of me as the only willful, flighty woman in the world.

Divorce was out of the question. I knew that as a Catholic Pierre would oppose it. While he humoured me by saying that if I wanted a divorce I should see a lawyer, I knew he would never co-operate in obtaining the three-year no-fault divorce available under Canadian law. What would be the point? He thinks one wife in a lifetime is quite enough and he has said to me many times, "You are my wife, you will always be my wife, and errant as you may be, nothing will ever change that." When I thought about divorce at all it was simply to reflect that if I ever wanted one I would simply have to wait the five years' separation required before I could apply on my own – either that or hand over full custody of the children, something I wouldn't consider. It was only much later that I learned that in the eyes of the law we were considered thoroughly married for as long as I lived at 24 Sussex, even though I slept in the attic. And to this day we are not even legally separated, despite what some people say.

But learning to cope with Pierre's dates wasn't easy. I was far more jealous than I thought I would be, and I was made furious from the start by Pierre's choice of women. Many of the women Pierre now took out were those who had come to 24 Sussex as friends during our marriage. Not only that – most were also career women in their own right. It all came back to his extremely old-fashioned attitude about women. For Pierre, women fell into three categories.

There were his female colleagues, and these he saw only as working companions and not as women, though many were also close friends. Then there were possible dates and here, like Edward VIII, he preferred actresses and starlets, glamorous women who were perfect for flirtations and candlelight dinners. Then there was his wife, and she had to be dependent, at home, and available. Though I knew his views, I couldn't help feeling envious of someone like Karen Kain, who was not only taken out by Pierre but also prized by him precisely because she was one of Canada's premier ballerinas. I couldn't help but grumble that if he had only allowed me my freedom to live and work we might never have become so estranged.

But there were also comic times, and these served, paradoxically, to bring us together. After one of my trips to New York in the autumn of 1977, I decided to cancel a few appointments and come home earlier, to fit in an extra weekend with the children. Expected on a Monday, my plane touched down in Ottawa the preceding Thursday. I phoned Pierre from the airport, was picked up and taken to 24 Sussex. I found Pierre ill at ease. He is a man who likes to know exactly what is happening; he also likes others to stick to their plans. I asked him what was wrong. He shifted about, embarrassed.

"Well, Margaret, I have a girlfriend coming for the weekend."

"That's fine," I said magnanimously. "You take her up to the lake. The children and I will stay here. After all, that's why I'm here."

I thought no more about it until I came in from shopping on Friday evening. There, hanging in the downstairs cupboard, was a hideous purple coat. Ugh, I thought, the jealous woman side coming out in me, she *sure* doesn't know how to dress. Then I saw, in the dining room downstairs, preparations for the dinner Pierre and I, in our heyday, used to have on Friday nights: lobster and champagne. *My* dinners. That didn't please me at all.

Upstairs I found Pierre packing, while the children rampaged around him. He was distinctly nervous. Suddenly I found the whole thing enormously funny: here I was, lying with my sons on the marital bed, while Pierre was getting all dolled up for a tête à tête up at the lake. After a while Pierre joined in the fun. And while we rolled about, howling with laughter, tickling the boys and making rude remarks, a happy family, there was his date downstairs, sitting primly in the drawing room waiting for the Prime Minister.

Pierre's date was Liona Boyd. I knew her well: I had frequently hired her to play classical guitar for visitors. Liona has pretty, fragile blond looks and wears Edwardian clothes – all lace and frills to enhance her image of classical gentleness. She isn't exactly bland, but she certainly wouldn't talk back to Pierre – although she's not above a little self-promotion. The following Monday I picked up a copy of *Maclean's* magazine and found a long interview with her in which she commented on her "relationship" with the Prime Minister. She had told the interviewer that the three boys were little darlings and that she had pet names for all of them. "And what about Margaret?" the interviewer had asked. "Oh," she had simpered. "I just do wish Margaret would get her head together." You foolish girl, I thought, I dare you to say that to my face. I wasn't surprised when I heard what she called her next album: *The First Lady of the Guitar*.

Liona Boyd wasn't the only one. I kept getting reports about Pierre's girls becoming ever more youthful – I used to tease him and say he would soon have a rival in Justin. Usually, Pierre and I were able to joke about it all, helped by my conviction all along that Pierre wasn't really serious about any of these women, that he loved to flirt but didn't for an instant believe that there would be any woman besides me in his life. If this sounds contradictory, I can only say that the situation was one of contradictions: Pierre and I love each other dearly, more dearly perhaps than we will ever love anyone else, but it

79

is not the love of a good marriage. The night of the Légers' ball, Pierre and his party came home early. Pierre was obviously in fine form. He came up to my room.

"Margaret, you know everyone here. Why don't you put on your robe and come down and join us."

I was feeling lonely, so was pleased to make an appearance. I asked what the evening had been like, and learned that Liona Boyd had played her guitar for the reception.

"Oh," I said wickedly, "so you had a mistress play?"

Pierre came back at me just as mischievously. "No Margaret, not one, but two."

It seems that a chanteuse friend of Pierre had been asked along to play as well, and what each can have made of it I have no idea.

While Pierre was adjusting to my comings and goings and his own return to semi-bachelorhood, he was not having the best of times politically. His popularity in the country had never really recovered from the heady late Sixties and early Seventies. His famous "bleeding hearts" remark, made at the height of the Laporte and Cross kidnappings, had labelled him callous and contemptuous and lost him forever the high regard of his former admirers on the intellectual left. No more was he Canada's champion of civil liberties. As well, there was the whole question of Quebec's move toward separatism and Pierre's passionate nationalism, his insistence on bilingualism, his refusal to tackle the alienation of the West. These were all issues that were eroding the place at the forefront of Canadian politics that rightfully he still felt to be his. An election was coming, but Pierre didn't seem to have the heart for it. His evasions were being branded as indecision; even Joe Clark, the leader of the opposition, took to mocking him for being "afraid to face the people."

Hostility against Pierre seemed to be growing on all

sides. Little as I tried to be involved, little as I tried to hear, it was impossible to avoid it all. Cab drivers became the bane of my life. There came a time when I could never seem to get into one without encountering a driver whose one mission in life seemed to be to slander Pierre. One day, in downtown Toronto, I had a particularly unpleasant experience.

We were bowling along when suddenly, without provocation, the driver launched into an attack on Pierre, calling him a tyrant and a dictator. I'm not one to stay silent, but then I didn't want a brawl either.

"I beg to differ," I said, trying not to lose my temper. "I think our Prime Minister is a wonderful man and that what he is doing is important for the future of Canada."

The driver paid no attention. "And what is more," he said, "he's a raving fag. For a few years he had us fooled with that lovely young wife Margaret but she's just a front. . . ."

"Stop this cab," I yelled. "I don't have to sit and listen to you. You're an ugly, bigoted old man."

I thrust some money into his hand; he tried to give it back, but by then I was in full flight: "Look," I said, "I don't have to take rides from people like you. Never."

I slammed the door and strode off, leaving him shaking his head in amazement. I was shaking a bit myself: of all the criticisms I've heard about Pierre over the years, the charge that he is gay is certainly the most unfounded and absurd.

How much Pierre's fading popularity was my fault I couldn't judge. But when I allowed myself to, I felt dreadfully guilty. During the election of 1974, I had thrown myself as far as I could into the political arena, not just doing my own part in campaigning, but counselling Pierre about the image he should have: more open, less arrogant, more approachable. I wondered now whether I should once again be making comments on what I saw was happening. But I was too disheartened to say much. Why should I bother when Pierre didn't really want my advice any more? I stuck to recommending which tie should go with which suit.

Many of the more malicious and manipulative journalists, I soon discovered, believed me to be Pierre's Achilles' heel. Unable to break through his aloof veneer of self-protection, they thought they could get at him through me. They were wrong. I did my best to avoid being exploited on his account by refusing interviews and staying home most of the time, so that I was not seen around. For his part, Pierre handled our brand of separation, my would-be career, his role with the boys, with utter grace and dignity. They jeered and taunted, but he would not be drawn out. As a result he ended up – on this front at least – looking like a winner.

The long weeks of the autumn of 1978 inched by. I came and went; the boys grew; Pierre and I became more and more unhappy in one another's company. On the surface we seemed to be handling the contradictions of such a relationship. Below it, I was becoming more and more bitter, the rage that was later to explode in such mental confusion building up within me.

Looking back on it, I now realize that my strongest single emotion at the time was one of resentment, resentment against Pierre over the life that he was forcing me, through his misconceived stinginess, to lead. For the terms he had stipulated – no money, and the boys to remain at 24 Sussex – were simply not fair, though I had neither the strength nor the clarity to see it at the time. On my more depressed days it seemed to me that I was being deprived of the best years of the boys' lives – and my own – by a bunch of nannies and a parsimonious man old enough to be my father.

All might have gone on this way, at least for a while longer, because I know now that my mind was being very severely buffeted, had it not been for an event that convinced me forever that, whatever I might feel for Pierre, his love for me was dead. It's perhaps surprising that it came to me as such a shock, but I have always deluded myself about such things.

At the end of 1978, realizing that I had a few weeks with no firm plans outside Canada, I decided to have my tonsils out. They had bothered me mildly for years, and my doctor had now convinced me that the time had come to have them removed. I went into Ottawa General Hospital, was horrified to find how painful the operation and ensuing weeks of recuperation turned out to be, then returned to convalesce at 24 Sussex. Unfortunately, this coincided with the Légers' farewell ball and the weeks of intense social preparation that preceded it, so I did not rest as I should have. While we had guests, I worked hard to make them comfortable. It was only once they had left that I realized how sick I was.

At midnight on a Friday night, I awoke in my attic room to find myself coughing blood. Terrified, I went downstairs to Pierre's room and asked him to call the doctor. For Pierre, Friday nights, the end of the working week, are sacred: not prepared to have his own ruined, he was loathe to disturb the doctor. He got out of bed, brought me a basin, which I soon filled with blood, and said that we should wait until morning to call the doctor. When I seemed better, he helped me back to my bed and returned to his own.

A couple of hours later, the bleeding started again. Once again I crawled to Pierre, begging him this time to call the doctor. He refused, brought me another basin and went back to bed. It didn't occur to me to wake anyone else; after all, I trusted Pierre implicitly. I held on until six, sick, bleeding and frightened. It was only then, when Pierre judged the moment right, that he consented to pick up the phone.

The doctor had been packing the car for a weekend on the ski slopes. Had we left it twenty minutes longer, he would have been gone. As it was, he was with us in ten minutes, took one look at my throat, called the ambulance and, pausing only to bawl out Pierre for his stupidity, rushed me to the nearest hospital. Several transfusions and another operation later, the hospital declared that I was out of danger. It was the fact that I might have died, and that Pierre was not interested enough to prevent it, that finished forever the committed love I once had for him.

Chapter Six
Publicizing Myself

On April 20, 1979, Paddington Press published my book, *Beyond Reason*. It was a moment I had been partly looking forward to, partly dreading, for many months. I believed that I had done an honest job, told the truth about my life as I saw it, but as the day approached for it to hit the world I began to fear that I had been too honest, gone too far. The advance publicity did nothing to reassure me: sensationalism, that was to be the order of the day.

I had agreed with John and Janet Marqusee that I would do a certain amount of promotion. Canada, where I already felt overexposed, was out of bounds because Pierre was by now fighting an election campaign. That left the United States and England.

The tour kicked off in London but it was not an auspicious start. Because the *Daily Express* had bought the serialization rights, I had agreed to be interviewed for a short television commercial promoting the excerpt. The interviewer, I was told, was a senior figure at the paper, but from the start I found his unkempt appearance and brash manner hard to stomach.

I remember the day well. The *Express* had rented or borrowed someone's apartment in Belgravia as a classy setting for the interview. But it was only half-furnished, so I felt as if we were sitting in a museum. And I didn't like the way that my interviewer chose to warm me up, before the cameras were rolling, by repeating, over and over again, "Do you smoke pot, Margaret? Tell me about pot. Have you had many experiences with pot?" rolling the words around in his mouth as if savouring them.

When I saw what the *Express* had done to the book, my spirits sank still lower: a messy job of cutting had distorted stories that in their totality made sense but, pruned, showed me up as self-centered and star mad. What I felt was so unfair was that I still regarded myself as brave in all the things I had faced up to in *Beyond Reason*, and here I was being made to feel ashamed, as if I had done something distasteful. Who cared, I was fast learning, about what I actually thought and felt? What the world wanted, was going to want out of me during my promotion tour, was sex, drugs and rock 'n' roll.

After the television commercial came a newspaper interview. I had been warned that Jean Rook of the *Daily Express* was bitchy and inquisitive: her reputation I soon discovered was too kind to her. With her bossy, horsey face plastered in makeup, and her graceless putdown manner, I found this doyenne of English women's journalism one of the most exasperating women I had ever met.

She can't have cared for me. During the interview she was ingratiating, full of interest in my exploits, redolent of charm. Later, when the piece came out, I saw that it was all buttering me up in order the better to slap me down. "She walked out on a Prime Minister," her article began. "Left her three little boys. Rocked the world with her weekend with the Rolling Stones. She's a self-confessed hippie who smokes pot, uses four-letter words and makes it obvious she doesn't wear a bra."

I did one more interview while I was in London. This was with the Canadian television programme, *W5*, and my clear understanding of the agreement was that the interview would be held until my book appeared in Canada. I felt quite pleased with that effort: the programme showed me looking good and there was nothing in it at all that could have conceivably changed the course of Canadian history. That it was to become one more item of trouble only revealed itself later.

And so, before tackling the States, I permitted myself a holiday. I couldn't go back to Canada: the election campaign was in full swing and I didn't want to meddle. Instead I accepted an offer from Jorge, the Peruvian racing driver I had met the summer before in London, to accompany him home to stay with his family and see something of South America.

I had already grown fond of his mother Dora during a visit she had made to London. She was a marvellous Peruvian-born woman of Viennese parents. Jorge and I spent a few days with her in Lima, then drove up into the mountains, the high Andes, for Easter. Being unlucky enough to hit an enormous local festival, we found every hotel full, so were forced to camp out. The presence in the car of a large gun that Jorge's Uncle Wolf, an ex-Nazi with a crewcut, had urged us to take with us, was not reassuring. Already I was finding Peru very alien.

Since it was dark by the time we decided to stop, all we could do was pick a spot and hope for the best. We settled on a sheltered plateau with a stream running alongside. As light dawned, we looked out of the windows and saw, looming high above us, an immense statue of Jesus Christ, arms outstretched in benediction. And then we looked around us: we had parked the car, we now saw, on rubble, and the full horror struck us that it was the rubble of a town recently erased by an earthquake. Shivering at the thought of all those ghosts beneath us, we drove hastily away.

On our return to Lima, Jorge announced that he had to go to Bolivia on business for a few days and so he arranged for me to visit Cuzco and the Machu Picchu ruins, accompanied by a close family friend, a girl known to them all as "little sister." She and I set off together by plane the next day but, to my astonishment, once she had installed me in a hotel in Cuzco and introduced me to some architect friends, she vanished, never to return.

Still, the holiday started well. I spent an enjoyable day among the Inca ruins with the architects, ending up at a remote farmhouse for a barbecue. Toward dusk, exhausted by the altitude, I hitched a ride from a girl called Mia who was driving with her three-year-old daughter back down the mountain to Cuzco, an hour or so away, having dropped her American husband and a party of trekkers on the Inca Trail. Mia was eight months' pregnant and she had two Afghan dogs in the back of the truck.

The road down followed a valley through the mountains. After we had rounded one bend I could see ahead of us a truck pulled over by the roadside. Mia began to slow down. As she did so, a child, a boy of about eight, darted into the road in front of us. I shouted out, Mia swerved and missed him. But then, fast on his heels, a second child ran into the road, never looking right or left. It was a little girl, and we hit her.

Mia put her foot hard on the brake, swerved violently, then took it off and accelerated even harder.

I couldn't figure out what she was doing. I grabbed the wheel, shouting at her to stop.

"I can't, you don't understand, I can't," she sobbed. Tears were pouring down her face, but she kept on going. "I'm too frightened. We have got to get help." Her daughter was wailing, with fear, between us. I felt sickened; uncomprehending. We careened through a village and drove on. Behind us, far up the mountain, I could see lights setting off in pursuit.

What seemed to me hours later we got into Cuzco. No

sooner had we turned the first corner than the police stopped the car, dragged us out into the road and led me one way and Mia another. I spoke no Spanish and none of the numerous police spoke English. They were not unkind, but I simply couldn't understand what they wanted. I gave them all my documents; they waved them away. I wrote down the name of my hotel; they shrugged. Three hours passed. Finally they drove me to an unknown street and stopped, pointing to a door. By now I was in a state of near hysteria.

I groped my way out of the car, pressed the bell indicated to me. At once it opened and there, to my overwhelming relief, stood Mia. She was calm, almost brusque.

"Thank goodness you've come. Can you lend me some money?"

Speechless, I looked in my purse, found one hundred and forty dollars, and handed it to her. "Aren't they going to arrest you?" I asked frantically.

She looked puzzled. "Oh, no," she replied. "That's not the way things work here."

Suddenly it all became clear. We were to bribe our way out. Only money, not the safety of the child, nor the immorality of not having stopped, counted. That's what the police had been waiting for.

That night, back at my hotel, I kept vomiting with shock. Next day, I caught the plane down to Lima. Sitting, waiting for takeoff, still shaking with horror but relieved to have escaped, I suddenly saw racing across the runway two police officers, gesticulating violently. My heart froze. It was obvious: they were coming for me. When they hauled off a poor Indian who was trying to accompany his mother I cried with relief.

Back in Lima I found that Jorge was in total disgrace for having allowed me to go off unaccompanied. But I didn't feel any better about Peru, particularly when I discovered that Mia's flight had been entirely sensible. Had we stopped, Dora explained to me, we would very probably have been stoned to death. Now, I longed to leave. Peru was a vastly different culture from mine, a violent place whose rules I could not follow. The little girl didn't die – but I couldn't stop asking myself: Who leaves a dying child by the roadside? As soon as I could book a flight I took off for New York. But it wasn't a good start to my promotion tour: I felt badly shaken, dazed and far from in control.

I reached New York toward the end of April to find the Paddington Press promotion team in full swing. The Marqusees had seemed lukewarm about English sales. In the States they turned into tigers. By now, however, I was learning the ropes of self-promotion fast. My humiliation at the hands of Jean Rook had convinced me to refuse other newspaper interviews – I would do only radio and television, where at least I could be certain that what I was quoted as saying I really had said.

We decided first of all to hit the major networks – and only prime-time national television. After all, I wasn't on what some poor authors have to suffer, a really vigorous selling spree. The first thing I discovered was that Suki Howard, American joint vice-president of Paddington, had been assigned to take care of me. I had been checked into the Carlyle, my favourite hotel. Paddington was picking up the tab and I was ready to go. I wasn't nervous of the cameras: one thing that had come from being Pierre's wife was that I was simply no longer afraid of crowds or publicity.

And then there was something heady about being so much in demand. I revelled in my lovely suite at the Carlyle, in the limousines ever ready for me at the door, in the baskets of red roses constantly arriving on my table. What's more, I could kid myself that I had finally made it: I wasn't dreaming of having work to do in New

York, I actually *had* it. As the offers poured in, a press agent friend said to me: "What you need, Margaret, is not a press agent, but a suppress agent."

My first show was on *Today*, the number-one American morning news programme. My interviewer was Jane Pauley, a likeable, sweet-as-they-come, cute sort of girl with whom I lunched a couple of days before our talk. We had joked about our names: her real Christian name is Margaret, and she was about to marry cartoonist Garry Trudeau. I told her: "You can have my name, with pleasure. Take it for all the good it will do you. It's yours."

On the air, we started well. Jane had a list of questions and, secure in the fine clothes I still had from my London high life, I felt on top of the world. If I had any reservations, it was about the time of day – seven forty-five in the morning – and I had been there at six. Mornings are not my best time. Then, casually, Jane asked:

"And what, Margaret, is the name of the man who ruined your marriage? The man you call your 'Southerner' in *Beyond Reason*?"

I made a joke of my answer. "I'm perfectly prepared," I told her, "to go beyond reason, but not beyond the contents of my book."

The interview over, I prepared to go. A producer came up, looking angry but distinctly apologetic. "There have been a few technical hitches," he told me. "Would you mind just doing the last few minutes again?" He called Jane off to one side.

When she returned to her chair, I saw immediately that she was flushed with embarrassment and clutching what was clearly a totally new list of questions. I couldn't, for a second, imagine what was coming. The cameras whirred, we started recording, and the questions began. This time there was no disguising the hostility. Who was the man? Why wouldn't I give his name?

91

Didn't everyone already know who he was? Who was I to be so secretive?

I rose to my feet. "Look Jane," I said, in front of five million viewers, "I just don't have to take this. This is your life, not mine." And I left.

There happened to be a photographer in the studio: the scene made the front pages. Jane Pauley, the girl from next door who is everyone's favourite interviewer, insults Mrs Trudeau on television. Whatever hesitations there might have been about promoting my book, it was now hot news. That night, a producer from *Today*'s main competitors, *Good Morning America*, called me at the Carlyle, his voice sugary with reassurance. "We were so sorry to hear of your bad experiences with *Today*," he said. "If you appear with us we'll certainly be most polite."

They were. Next morning Hugh Downs, the anchor-man, gave me the sweetest interview I have ever had. It was also the most boring – to hear us talk, you would think that I had never done anything in my life except love my husband and raise my kids. But by now, twelve million Americans had seen me on their morning screens.

The controversy didn't die at once. After all, Jane Pauley had been right about one thing: the most tantalizing part of the book was in fact my secret lover, and by now every paper in town was spreading the story: "Rumour has it that Margaret Trudeau's Southerner is none other than Teddy Kennedy. . . . " Were they right? It's a secret I intend to keep.

Next, in New York in early May, came the *Phil Donahue* show, the most demanding of my appearances, live in Madison Square Garden before five thousand people. Had it not been for my past training with Pierre I would never have stood up to it. The victim is put on a chair in the middle of blinding lights in the well of an auditorium, surrounded by spectators, who shout out questions. The chair swivels, so that you can at least face, if not see, your tormentors.

And torment it was: "Who's your lover? Have you abandoned your children? What are your values, Mrs Trudeau, that you can so easily walk out on a man fighting a political election? How can you justify hurting your family in this way?"

For a while I struggled. I tried to answer each question as it came pounding down at me. I said I didn't think it was hurting my family. I said I believed a woman had to have courage to make choices and that some were bound to be painful. They were nearly all women, these hateful questioners, and at last I could stand it no longer. After one haranguing vixen sitting high above had been punching at me for what seemed hours, I swung my chair around in the opposite direction to indicate such rubbish was over. That silenced her. Phil Donahue was a nice man, but he had not been prepared to cope with such aggression.

My last appearance was probably the most enjoyable. Merv Griffin invited me to join Liv Ullman, Hermione Gingold and Lucille Ball's daughter, Lucy Arnaz, on a talk show. No torments here: just questions leading to anecdotes and a lot of good stories from each of us.

All in all, New York was a success. My children had joined me for a week at the Carlyle and we were much feted all over town. Like me, the boys loved the limousines. Even the injunction against *W5* couldn't spoil it. *W5*, which had prerecorded its interview with the stipulation that it not be used until after the publication of my book in Canada, now announced its intention of airing it immediately. Evidently my remarks were deemed to be of "national interest." Even in my somewhat overexcited state, my mind whirling with all that was happening to me, I was absolutely clear that I had told *W5* no major indiscretion at all, and certainly no state secrets of a kind to jeopardize national security. A little gossip, yes; political dynamite, no. Quite apart from anything else I didn't know any.

And so Paddington Press and Optimum of Montreal (my publisher for the French-language edition in Quebec and France) filed an injunction against *W5*— and spent an enormous amount of money on lawyers, a sum I only discovered later Paddington deducted from my earnings. As it was, we won the case. It was good for my morale, too, because it proved me to be not the flakey, irresponsible threat to national security they were trying to make me out to be, but a professional writer promoting a book, meeting serious contracts and deadlines.

I needed the reassurance. ████████████████ syndicate had bought the American serialization rights and all across the United States posters blared my story. Only it wasn't my story: it was a distorted, truncated, vicious adaptation of my story, and it made me out to be petulant and self-centered. "Shock-a-page best seller." "Sensational stories." "Margaret Trudeau tells all." "Drug abuse, sexual freedom...." The posters held nothing back.

New York promotion had proved so successful, however, that even the Marqusees now agreed to let me skip Chicago and Dallas and make my way straight to Los Angeles. I was glad of the break. On the outside I still appeared in control and unflappable. Inside, the combination of my experience in Peru and the public reaction to *Beyond Reason* made me feel I was being pulled apart in a thousand pieces, as if the world had suddenly grown devouring and hostile. I have never taken criticism well and the growing image of me frivolously dominating the media with my whines and hysteria, while Pierre was battling for his political life, did not make an attractive spectacle.

It was not, I was fast learning, that the public seemed to mind about the drugs and the frivolity, or even the infidelity. Many others had done that before me. What they appeared to object to was the fact that I had dared to rock the boat, question the sanctity of public life. Public figures, my critics seemed to be saying, are public property, and public property must be above reproach. I found this shocking. Why, I wondered bitterly, should I be treated this way? I was a person, not a robot.

As it turned out, the promotion side was only to be the smallest of my California preoccupations. Just before leaving New York for the West Coast I had spent a last evening at Studio 54. Sometime during the night I had bumped into Ryan O'Neal, who took my telephone number and, hearing that I was coming west, suggested that we have dinner together when I arrived. One of the telephone messages waiting for me at the Beverly Hills Hotel was from him: "Mr. O'Neal will be picking you up for dinner at seven thirty." The final accolade of the high life: a date with the most handsome and desirable of film stars. It was something of a joke, but I fell for it.

Ryan arrived in a taupe-coloured open Rolls, wearing his by now legendary Hawaiian silk shirt and jeans. Dinner in a Polynesian restaurant was the start of one of the shortest-lived, most exciting and absurd of affaires – a one-week stand of Hollywood romance. Ryan's house stands on what used to be John Barrymore's estate, a flat bungalow surrounded by wooden fences, high up in the canyons. In the spring of 1979 he had just finished making *The Main Event* with Barbra Streisand, and considered himself quite a boxer. He was charming, but he was also spoiled and vain, and made much of his workouts in the gymnasium he had set up behind the house.

The house itself was magnificent, built to converge on a central courtyard around a swimming pool. His bedroom was decorated in dark reds and Liberty prints and there was an immense canopy over the bed, which was covered with the finest linen sheets. Tatum, his daughter, lived with him, in a suite of her own rooms adjoining his. She was away during my week's idyll.

I liked Ryan, but I found him shallow and I knew perfectly well that he represented everything that was wrong about the way I lived: the jet-setting, the wild life. By being with him at all I was living up to the very reputation I wished so hard to escape. We didn't have a very sensational time – but we had fun. He had a nice maid who brought us breakfast in bed and told me that I was the only person she had met, apart from Ryan, who never, ever, wanted to get up. We rarely went out. When I wasn't at a studio and we weren't in bed we lay by the pool and talked, not high life, but domesticity, often about our children, his and mine, and how they were turning out. I found the nicest side of him was his obvious devotion to his children.

I stayed with him a week, sneaking back to the Beverly Hills Hotel in the early mornings or during the day, in time to dress and turn up for the television interviews arranged for me. Because my mind was so completely elsewhere the promotion itself seemed to pass without event. I have little memory of it now.

What I do remember, though, with a certain sense of embarrassment, is the day that I returned from *The Mike Douglas Show* and banged on Ryan's door to be let in, only to be told to go away. He had his son there watching television and didn't want me to meet him. Hitching up my short red leather skirt, I scaled the incredibly high wall around his house, teetering on my very high-heeled black suede pumps, with my chauffeur watching in amazement. When I dropped down on the other side Ryan was far from pleased, though he soon started preening under my insistent attentions. That's what seemed to have happened to me with Ryan: I went right over the wall, carried away by the Hollywood nights and my image of myself as a sort of female Errol Flynn, with Ryan as my leading man.

By the end of the week I had had enough of it. Ryan's conceit, his self-obsession – he was too much for me. Everything was too much for me. I was strung out, exhausted and sick of all the Hollywood hype. In hindsight one incoherent incident sums up for me my confusion and frustrated impulsiveness.

Driving back to the studio one day, I told my chauffeur that I was hungry and he said that he knew of an excellent takeout Japanese restaurant. He was right; the food was delicious. I was sitting in the back of the car munching rice balls and raw fish when I noticed that Sunset Strip, down which we were driving, was plastered with posters announcing *The Main Event*, Ryan's film.

"Stop, stop," I shouted out.

The chauffeur slammed on the brakes.

Seizing the remains of my lunch, I jumped from the car, lined myself up in front of a poster showing Ryan and Barbra Streisand and, moulding the food into a soft ball in my hand, let fly.

It was a bull's eye. Yards above me, for all Hollywood to see, stared out Ryan's youthful features – splattered with rice and fish.

I climbed back into the car. "That's for you, Ryan O'Neal," I said happily to myself, relishing a feeling of sweet revenge. I never saw him again.

The one show that really alarmed me was Tom Snyder's, mainly because he was away and a well-known dragon was to be my interviewer. The talk show is aired live at one in the morning. I called for my limousine and made my way alone out to the studio, where I would have been miserable had it not been for the reassuring presence of two now-forgotten Australians promoting something of their own. They nursed me on to the show, sat around waiting for the postmortem and delivered me back to the hotel.

Meanwhile Suki Howard, the Paddington representative, set about arranging a few more appointments for me. Celeste Fremon of *Playgirl* magazine, a pretty sleazy magazine more famous for its nude male centrefolds than for its witty interviews, wanted to come and talk to me. At first I refused. I had turned down the more serious *Playboy*. Why accept this? But in the end I agreed.

The afternoon I was to leave for New York a nice, healthy, all-California girl turned up at my hotel room and introduced herself as Celeste. From the start we got along well, so well in fact that I missed my plane. "Don't worry," said Celeste. "Take a later one. And since you're here, why don't you come with me to the celebrity fashion show that Jane Fonda and Jon Voigt are hosting at the Beverly Wilshire Hotel ballroom? I have two ringside seats."

I was delighted: a few more days in Hollywood, why not? Nothing to make me hurry home. It was a delightful show highlighting the best of young Hollywood, the models in wild kinky clothes by the newest and most exciting of American designers, dancing and roller disco-ing. After lunch Celeste took me backstage to meet Jane Fonda and Jon Voigt. Walking back down the corridor, rather enjoying the models and the clothes and the whole crazy feeling of the event, I caught sight of someone I had not seen in a long while.

I was wearing dark glasses so I moved over to stand by him, then pretended to trip. As I stumbled into him the man grabbed hold of me, saying in tones and words still extraordinarily familiar to me: "Don't bother to apologize darling." It was Jack Nicholson.

Jack was with his producer friend Lou Adler, and the four of us – Celeste was tagging along – arranged to meet in the Polo Lounge half an hour later. I needed to see Jack alone: he and Ryan are old friends/enemies, so I felt I had to tell him of my rather sordid affair before he heard it from anyone else.

I whispered to Jack that I had to speak to him.

"Certainly, my darling," he said, and led me off to the men's washroom, where I perched up on the toilet seat so that no one coming in would be able to see my legs.

A minute after we closed the door the outer doors banged open and a heavy man, wearing orange trousers by the look of the ankles, came into the room. He did nothing, simply stood about waiting. He knew something fishy was going on.

Having held our breath for what seemed like hours, we finally could stand it no longer and came sheepishly out.

Far from lecturing us, the hotel detective, for so he was, was extremely civil: "Ah it's you Mr Nicholson," was all he said. "I thought it might be a couple of fags."

At the Beverly Wilshire Hotel anything else, it seems, goes.

Jack invited us all back to his house in the hills. Lou Adler and Celeste came for a while, then left. I stayed, drawn once more by Jack's irresistible sneering charm as he said: "Hey honey, come and try my Jacuzzi." The Jacuzzi alone, as it turned out, was worth it. It was perched on the edge of his property, as large as a swimming pool, carved out of rock and surveying the whole San Fernando Valley. We lay in it drinking champagne. When we weren't there we watched movies in his screening room.

I knew Angelica was still in his life and Jack soon told me that her sister Allegra was coming to see him the next day. It was a horribly brief interlude, but I could not turn it down. As it happened, another of Jack's girls, a young English girl called Rachel Ward, turned up first. To save Jack's reputation – Where was mine, I wondered? – I had to change quickly into an elegant silk dress, hide my suitcases, double around to the front while he engaged her in conversation, and ring the doorbell, pretending I was merely dropping in for tea.

The last I saw of Jack was later that afternoon when an old friend, Brian Wilson, came to pick me up. At least I went out in style: Brian Wilson is a tall handsome man of over six feet who arrived driving his Jensen and wearing white silk pajamas. How was Jack to know he was no more than a good friend? As I stepped into his open sports car, I looked back and saw Jack standing in the street, pulling at what little hair he has on the top of his head and staring after me with total perplexity.

I reached New York the night of the Canadian elections. The six weeks I had been away were not good ones for Pierre. He had had no choice but to call an election with only four weeks left of a five-year term, but the cards had been stacked against him and in any case he had chosen to play them wrong. Canadians were sick of their charismatic Prime Minister; they had had enough of his arrogance, his pride, his increasingly lofty condescension, and as the campaign picked up momentum they made their displeasure felt.

But Pierre was not open to advice and the attitude he chose to take turned out to be hopelessly insensitive to the mood of the country. The voters might still have been wooed by a show of modesty. All they got was impervious rejection. So while Joe Clark covered the country with his bonhomie, Pierre hardly bothered to move around or co-operate with journalists, making it perfectly clear that he thought Joe was no match for him, and that he had nothing to fear. It was all gold for Joe Clark: all he had to do was sit around and pick up the anti-Trudeau vote.

Early on the evening of May 22, 1979, it became obvious that Pierre was going to lose. I had made a conscious

100

decision not to return to Ottawa in time for the results because I had a strong feeling that I had no business being there. I had played no part in the campaign and didn't want, now, to draw attention to myself, to become a late media event. Nor did I have any desire to vote: I was still feeling extremely rebellious about politics.

So I spent the evening alone in a New York apartment belonging to friends who had gone out to some formal reception. It had never occurred to me that Pierre was not going to win. I knew the campaign had gone badly – but for him to lose? to Joe Clark? I turned on the television. It was then that the full horror of what was happening began to strike me, and I wished bitterly that I had been at Pierre's side.

Not believing what I heard, I phoned friends in Ottawa for more news, more results, *different* results. It was not just defeat; it was humiliation, pure and simple. Pierre himself had been re-elected – but fourteen members of his cabinet had lost their seats.

When my friends came back I was ready for murder: I might no longer love Pierre, but I felt stricken by his defeat, and the shame, hurt and humiliation were mine just as much as his. I saw doom all around me. I couldn't believe this had happened. It was Pierre himself who confirmed it to me. Just before he went to make his resignation speech he spoke to me on the phone. "Oh yes," he said. "It's true, quite true. We're out."

I took a bottle of champagne from the fridge and tried to open it with my teeth until my friends, who had just returned, seized it from my mouth. The cork shot off into the ceiling. A minute more and it would have blasted into the roof of my mouth. I was too mortified to care. Then, against all their advice, I insisted on going out to Studio 54.

It was there that the press found me, dancing the night rapturously and callously away, the gayest, most indifferent person in the world. And it was as such that they portrayed me to the world next day: dancing, as it were, with my "naked midriff" and my "dishevilled hair," over my husband's political pyre. They could have had no idea how I felt inside.

Next morning I was horribly ashamed. I also had flu. Celeste Fremon showed up in New York and called, begging for a last half-hour of interview to complete her story. When I refused, she protested friendship, said she would bring me food and try to console me for what had happened.

That she brought her tape recorder with her was something I didn't really notice. Nor, in my sickness, did I bother to ask her to leave the room when Pierre finally called from Ottawa and we had a long, emotional telephone conversation. He tried to help me accept the defeat, understand it. Paradoxically it was not me comforting Pierre, but him me, in a fatherly, brave way. We talked for about twenty minutes, discussing intimate details about the future, the children, what had to be done, even my guilt about what had happened. Pierre kept telling me that I was not to blame; I kept repeating that I was. Celeste Fremon heard it all.

A happy evening at Studio 54 with two friends, the LOVE STORY couple Ali McGraw and Ryan O'Neal. (*R. Manning/Sygma*)

I borrowed a hat from a fellow dancer at Studio 54.
(*Wide World Photos*)

My last night ever at Studio 54.

Yasmin Aga Khan visits me in Ottawa.
(Bill Brennan)

Being interviewed by Phil Donahue was a little like being part
of the Spanish Inquisition. *(Wide World Photos)*

With Eri, my delightful Japanese interpreter, opening a club in
Tokyo. *(Wide World Photos)*

My sister Janet and I with Mr Tanabe, a writer with a bent for
all that's pleasurable.
(Courtesy Margaret Trudeau)

I was filled with admiration for Linda Griffiths' performance in her play MAGGIE & PIERRE. *(Glen E. Erikson/Talonbooks)*

Michel, Justin and Sacha. (© *Sherman Hines*)

Shopping in Ottawa. (*Russell Mant/Ottawa Citizen*)

In the northern town of Athabasca I speak to a fund-raising group.

At the premiere of KINGS AND DESPERATE MEN with Jim Johnson. *(CP Photo)*

Photographing Duane Bobick at the Joe Lewis gym was one of my assignments for PEOPLE Magazine. *(Courtesy Margaret Trudeau)*

Chapter Seven
Moving Out

A week after the election I recovered my spirits and my health sufficiently to return to Ottawa. I was determined not to go home until I could cope with what was to come, until I was cheerful enough to comfort Pierre, not plague him with my own disappointment. As it turned out, I found him surprisingly resilient, even joking about his downfall and totally resolved not to let anyone see how crushed he was underneath. I was in Ottawa in time for the ceremony at which he had to transfer power to the incoming Prime Minister. On Monday, June 4, a beautiful spring-like gentle day, Pierre drove himself over to Rideau Hall in his own Mercedes and lunched with the Governor General to hand over the symbol of power, the Great Seal of Canada. As he left, he turned to shout to reporters waiting on the steps: "I feel free."

Whether or not for Pierre it was really liberation, I couldn't help feeling our banishment intensely. It was partly that I felt very sorry for Pierre who I knew, behind that stern and cheery exterior, was mortified by what had happened. But I minded for me too, and for us as a family. I felt it was deeply sad that we were suddenly going to be turned out of a house that everyone agreed I had turned from a dreary unwelcoming official residence into a splendid and elegant house. Even though I knew we were only political tenants, I couldn't imagine being thrown so peremptorily out of the nest where I had nurtured my three babies, where I had presided over so many official functions, where I had moulded, with infinite patience and many mishaps, such an efficient staff.

And of course somewhere inside me, though I tried hard to fight it, was the prickling realization that I was partly to blame for Pierre's defeat. Even my ostrich attitude toward all press comment on my life had not quite protected me from the question that had gone around Ottawa in the days leading up to the election: "Has Pierre Trudeau's private life affected his judgment? Is a man who has spent eight years married to a woman like Margaret actually capable of leading Canada?" The "Margaret factor," I had surreptitiously read in one paper, had been widely regarded as a possible decider of the results. As an election issue there were days when it topped the one million unemployed, inflation rising to over ten percent and Canada's worries about energy.

What *had* I done, with my wild behaviour, my terrible indiscretions, my freedom trips and spending sprees? Had I actually cost Pierre the leadership? What could he think of me? Characteristically, Pierre never uttered the least reproach. The defeat, he assured me, was entirely his own responsibility. This was typical of his own particular brand of generosity for Pierre, so stingy when it comes to money, is also the most tolerant person I have ever met. Nor did his colleagues seem to blame me, though I sometimes wondered whether it wasn't only their manners and innate niceness that prevented any reproach from showing on their faces.

But it was impossible for me not to brood. In the heightened state of tension and excitement I was still in from my promotion tour, my frightening experience in Peru and my fleeting affaires with Jack and Ryan, I felt increasingly distraught, increasingly unsure that I could hold onto myself much longer. To avoid facing up to any of this, I turned myself doggedly to the coming move.

I put into abeyance all decisions about our future as a family, though I had never recovered my trust in Pierre after the night of my tonsils hemorrhage. It wasn't that I now believed we might get together again: simply that I was too numb, and Pierre too preoccupied by defeat, to go over the same old questions again.

Long before the ballot papers were finally cleared away, before Canadians had had time to realize they had a new Prime Minister and before, as a family, we had had time to lick our wounds, the Clarks made their triumph plain. Not just their satisfaction with political victory – that was understandable enough – but their intention to get the new order moving fast. In the week before I returned to Ottawa, Maureen McTeer (though wife of the incoming Prime Minister she was reluctant to bear his name, something I found absurd) had visited 24 Sussex with her decorator to take a look at what she was about to inherit. Having surveyed the official rooms, she had asked Pierre if she could see the top floor. Somewhat to her surprise, Pierre had refused. It wasn't just a reluctance to let her see my personal things: he had no intention of letting her get a glimpse of how we had been conducting our private lives.

I had never had much to do with the Clarks, but what little I had seen of them had not endeared them to me. Despite his somewhat goofy looks and his fake John Diefenbaker manner, Joe is not a bad man: he has a kindly and courteous manner that makes him seem older than his age. A "wimp" – that's what people called him. A good political organizer, I had no doubt of that, but a prime minister? Better, surely, president of the Conservative Party. Maureen is simply not my sort of woman: bouncy, worthy, humourless and now riding high, a girl from rural Ontario was how I had always seen her, and a keenly ambitious one at that. Intelligent. Very cold. I dreaded what I feared would be a series of putdown encounters at which she would parade her apparent dedication and hint at my own guilt. What I couldn't have realized was how trivial our exchanges would be.

We had just one conversation, over the telephone before we moved out of 24 Sussex. Hearing from Mrs Bennett, the housekeeper, that Maureen had declared her intention of making a lot of changes, I thought I should at least let her know that many of the things we had installed were of considerable rarity and value and that, as they belonged to the nation, they should not be dumped or hidden away in a room at the public works department. At first she seemed quite dismissive, making it plain for instance that the Italian velvet that I had ordered specially to cover the main sofa would have to go (she covered it instead in navy blue corduroy). But her appreciation for my interior decorating clearly grew as she discovered what it all cost.

At the beginning of July Pierre, Justin, Sacha, Michel and I moved over to Stornoway, the official residence of the leader of the opposition. As a house it is not distinguished: a square, grey, stucco house with no grandeur, no view, no feeling and no elegance – in short, no redeeming feature except for the sun porch, and even that was marred. A skunk had lived so long underneath it that its smell had totally permeated the wood. Inside, Stornoway was a nightmare. It was, in fact, so dreadful in appearance and content that we could only think that Maureen and Joe had made it that way as a sort of ploy, a gambit to use to indicate their frugality.

To start with, it was horribly dirty. Garbage was stacked knee high in every room – at 24 Sussex we had left no wastepaper basket unemptied – and it took three days for the garbage to be cleared. The bathtubs and sinks had not been cleaned in days; one of the toilets was blocked.

Nothing at all had been done to enliven the very meagre features the house possessed: each of the nineteen or so small pokey rooms was more depressingly painted and furnished than the last. A musty, greyish brown had been made the dominating colour; the basically pleasant wood floors had been firmly covered over with linoleum or dingy wall-to-wall; the wallpaper was of the cheapest and fraying at the edges; and in the dining room Maureen had put gold-coloured synthetic grass cloth. There were no curtains anywhere and the bathrooms were cobbled together in a makeshift way out of little bits of what appeared to be old kitchen linoleum. No feminine touch: no elegance or pride. As I walked around, I could have wept for my Italian wall coverings and matching silk curtains.

Furthermore, Stornoway didn't even work properly. Inspectors from the federal public works department, which I soon consulted, were horrified when they came on a tour of inspection. One of the duties of the people who inhabit these official residences is to keep them in perfect working order. The inspectors told me that the Clarks had always maintained that everything was functioning excellently, and so they had not been near the place for years. The roof leaked and needed to be repaired; the furnace had to be replaced, the floors mended, the walls replastered. So furred up were the pipes that the water flowing from them was soon declared undrinkable. I was not altogether surprised when I found among the garbage a large cardboard box containing many years of McTeer family photographs: throwing it out, I could only conclude, was Maureen's gesture of farewell to a life happily left behind.

Meanwhile the Clarks had settled down to revamping 24 Sussex. Pierre and I had agreed to take the minimum with us and to leave them the residence as it stood: furniture, pictures, plates. Only our personal linen came with us. I had rather yearned for the burnt orange Ginori plates, but at the last minute felt it would be too mean to take them, as they matched so perfectly the Fortuny wall covering in the dining room, especially as Maureen assured me that she would be leaving it all as it was.

She didn't. Within days I started hearing of the pillage, the rape, of 24 Sussex. All that was beautiful, all that I had chosen with such loving care, was now ripped out and replaced with all that was most mediocre. The full-length yellow silk curtains were chopped in two, to dangle aimlessly in midair. My Fortuny covering was ripped off and replaced with beige paper, while above it the elaborate ceiling, which I had taken such pains to leave very plain, stood out in gaudy gold. (She told friends that the Fortuny orange was too like the Liberal colour – red – to bear, yet the dining room of Stornoway featured pumpkin orange paint.)

Next, Maureen removed the neutral carpet that I had chosen for the ground floor and replaced it in the hall with huge patches of the most suburban black and white linoleum. To go with it, she decided to jazz up the reception rooms with paisley slipcovers. And while she kept the order of the rooms much as we had arranged them, she decided to turn what had been our formal and charming library into a sort of emperor's anteroom, where courtiers visiting the Prime Minister could sit and drink coffee out of A & W coffee mugs from an ever-bubbling cafeteria machine. Soon, I could no longer decide whether I was more depressed by what I had inherited or by what Maureen McTeer was vandalizing in my past.

The staff fared little better than the furnishings. Hildegard (the maid), Ruth (our kitchen cook) and Rosa (the laundress) opted to come with us to Stornoway. They had worked for us too long, they said, to want a change now. Mrs Bennett departed when Maureen told her to start waiting at table; another maid quit the day she was instructed to serve meals as well as clean the bathrooms. The maids chafed under a regime as confused as it was impractical. Pierre and I had always been careful not to give two official lunches – one of his and one of mine – on the same day, just as we had taken care to have the staff on in shifts, and give them generous weekend leave. Maureen expected constant service. Her brand of egalitarianism also took the form of a sort of mucking-in, directionless policy, expecting everyone to chip in and help. Used to hierarchy and routine, it was hardly surprising that some staff felt at a loss.

Only Yannick seemed impervious to the chaos, even if he resented his superb French cuisine being replaced by menus straight off the back of cans. Of course it meant less work: spaghetti bolognese rather than fish pâté, boeuf stroganoff and raspberry flan for forty. But even he objected to the constant presence of the Clark child, Catherine, then just two. Maureen did not believe in nannies and had found Catherine a place at a local day-care centre. The trouble was that the hours were not very long, and that since Maureen herself was still working hard as a law student, the child spent most of the day at 24 Sussex without much supervision.

Only Harrington Lake escaped Maureen's depradations. So busy was she wreaking havoc at 24 Sussex that she took barely a glance at the country house and decided to leave that until later – mercifully, for it saved it. The Clarks did use the house occasionally, but in a very different way. While we had always considered it a family refuge, they saw it in terms of an alternative party place, and drove up mainly to give receptions.

Meanwhile Pierre and I were struggling to adapt to Stornoway. For the first six months, this meant living on

117

a building site, as plumbers, plasterers and carpenters trooped in and out trying to put the place in shape. Once again, Pierre and I agreed to have separate rooms, and once again I opted for one of the servant's rooms on the second floor because it was next door to the children's playroom. Pierre took the master suite on the first floor.

But our lives could not have been more different from the days of official splendour. Ruth cooked, but plainly, a far cry from Yannick's rich food. Her simplicity of style suited Pierre well. He was preoccupied with a need to economize. He was paying the food bills from his own pocket now, not the public one, and took a decidedly frosty attitude when I ordered steak for dinner.

The boys survived the move best. For one thing they were able to enjoy a sense of freedom long denied them by watchful police guards. Pierre and I took turns walking them to school and we got some satisfaction out of adapting and improving three little bedrooms for them – Pierre himself paid for the furnishings.

But Pierre, I soon noticed, was taking the defeat badly. His early insouciance was fast vanishing under frustration and boredom. When, on the night of the election, I had rather drunkenly told reporters: "He is going to be the greatest leader of the opposition, not only because he is going to fight for individual freedom but because he's going to fight boringness," I had no notion of how powerless Pierre's life would be. He had long been used to the feel and machinery of power: overnight it had been seized from him. Many of his aides had gone, his RCMP special security guards had gone. The automatic status, so long his by right, had vanished. And he had lost the one place he really loved, Harrington Lake.

It was not surprising he was depressed, particularly as he had to watch from the sidelines as Clark made mistake after mistake over issues that Pierre had so painfully woven into shape. Soon after his election, for example,

Clark decided to transfer the Canadian Embassy in Israel from Tel Aviv to Jerusalem, thereby alienating the whole Arab world. When he stopped to think about the enormous Canadian contracts in Saudi Arabia, he had to renege on his promise, to the extreme disappointment of the Israelis.

Pierre had kept his office; Joe Clark had turned it down on the grounds that it was too small. But I found that he went there less and less, preferring to delegate minor decisions that fall to opposition leaders to his senior aides and vanish into the country. He grew a beard. He went off on holiday with the boys to Quebec and Nova Scotia. Then he joined a canoeing party down the Hanbury and Thelon rivers in the North West Territories. In the autumn he ventured deep into Tibet for, no doubt, serious contemplation. I wasn't sure how much longer he would last in politics.

In August, while Pierre was canoeing, I took the children to Vancouver to stay with my parents. One day my father answered the telephone: "Mr Sinclair," asked a strange voice, "could you tell me something about your daughter Margaret's abortion?"

The shock, to my family, was total; they knew nothing at all about it.

For a minute, I thought the caller must be bluffing. But then I remembered: Celeste Fremon. New York, the day after the election when she arrived at my hotel so sweetly bearing fruit and asked me why I had so many bruises (I was still recovering from the blood transfusions after my tonsilectomy). In my feverish confusion and self-pity I associated the easy bruising with my RH negative blood problem and I told her it had all been caused by my abortion. And then I kept on talking. . . .

And now, here it all was, in *Playgirl* magazine. I had, according to the interview Celeste had transcribed, had an abortion at seventeen at the hands of a drunken doctor, and next day flushed the foetus down the toilet of the department store where I worked, having become pregnant during an affaire with the captain of my college football team. . . . According to the story I had also told her, among dozens of other revelations, that I would always love Senator Kennedy "very, very deeply" and that I had spent a night with Ryan O'Neal.

In a long line of disasters and indiscretions this interview was certainly the worst. There was absolutely nothing I could say in my own defence. "How are you going to live the rest of your life?" my mother asked me acidly. How indeed? My father sat silent in reproach. Pierre looked bitterly disappointed. No one could have made me feel worse than I already did: a traitor to Pierre, a slut in the eyes of the world. I knew then that I had reached my lowest point and that there was no going back.

Chapter Eight
The Final Break

Sitting bleakly in my mother's living room in Vancouver, feeling like a small bad little girl, I reviewed my position. It did not look good. When I sorted out the tangle of arrangements and plans from the emotional chaos precipitated by my indiscretions – now once again front-page news in the Canadian papers – I saw that I no longer really had a choice. Whatever love Pierre had still felt for me up to that day was now dead: there was no redeeming the *Playgirl* article.

In fact, I don't really know how I would ever have been able to look anyone in the eye again had it not been for an encounter with Jeanie Southam, the mother of an old friend of mine and a tough woman with a sharp tongue who, as part of a family of newspaper proprietors, was well versed in my escapades. I had gone to see her daughter Stephanie on Vancouver Island knowing I would run into Jeanie, dreading a lecture. Hardly able to meet her eyes, I slunk down on a chair on the beach by her side.

Jeanie startled me, dismissing my self-obsessive guilt. "Oh come on Margaret," she said briskly. "Put your chin up. Everyone's done things they shouldn't have. I've done a lot I regret. It's just that no one ever found out. So buck up."

Celeste Fremon's article, and the reactions of all those around me, also did something else. The whole event now made me realize with extreme clarity that I was really on my own, that I was no longer beholden to others for my actions nor were they responsible for me. I could, at last, have some say in my own future, in actually designing the sort of life that suited me best. Perhaps writing *Beyond Reason* had played its part there too: analyzing a life, even as brief as mine had been until then, is a very maturing process. Going over the events and decisions I had made and trying to work out the steps that led to them had, quite simply, led me to view them differently and, sometimes, with less guilt. Grown up, I could leave Pierre. Not just could, but would.

My first reaction to this sudden clarity was characteristically scatty. Without thinking through the implications I decided to settle in Vancouver, retreat as it were into childhood, live in an apartment near my parents and begin again. I gave little thought to the fact that almost three thousand miles separate Vancouver from Ottawa, that whatever else the immediate future held, it was not custody of my children, and that since Pierre was adamant that there were no concessions to be made on that score, I would have to go to them, for they would not be allowed to come to me.

I found unexpected support (only unexpected because at that stage I didn't feel that I could *expect* any help from anyone) in the shape of a few good friends in Ottawa. We called ourselves the Gang of Five – my friends Jane Faulkner, Nancy Pitfield, Gro Southam, Rosemary Shepherd and I. They knew me well enough to know I needed help and it turned out they had been waiting only for Pierre's move to Stornoway to talk to him about me. While he was Prime Minister, understandably, they had felt they shouldn't really interfere. Now that Pierre was once again without the extreme pressures of office, our personal life had descended to an ordinary level.

When I returned to Ottawa from Vancouver Jane and Hugh Faulkner offered me an alternative home to Stornoway. They were between nannies and the bedroom the last girl had vacated now became my refuge. The Faulkners understood my feelings perfectly. Hugh, who had served in Pierre's cabinet and been a member of Parliament for fourteen years, had lost his seat in the election and was now looking for a job, and Jane shared my sense of humiliation and anger over what had happened. What was more, she felt that Pierre was now intimidating me. She was determined to do what she could to protect me.

Then there was Nancy Pitfield, the wife of Pierre's cabinet secretary Michael, who had also lost his job after the election and was now teaching at Harvard. Before they moved down to Boston Nancy went to see Pierre. She told him that he had become quite blind to my unhappiness, that she seriously believed that the time had come for the two of us to part and that the least he could do was to help me start again, for I *needed* a home. "Enough is enough," she said firmly.

Pierre, who reported this conversation to me later, didn't like this sort of talk at all. When I questioned him about what Nancy had said, he merely shrugged: "She thinks you're crazy. All your friends think you're crazy. They know you're out of your mind."

It was a malicious thing to do. Until I had the courage to question Nancy about this – and when I did she denied it furiously – I brooded anxiously over the words. Was I perhaps crazy? Was that why I behaved so badly?

Looking back, everything seems so much clearer. The point was not that I was mad but that I and so many of my friends were examining our lives and finding them wanting. And so we were all abandoning ship, changing our lives, and none of it was easy. My friend Gro, a Norwegian who was recently divorced from Hamilton Southam, was trying to make up her mind to take her children back to Europe and study at Christie's auction house in London. In her own way she was in as much turmoil as I.

It was so very, very comforting to be reminded that it wasn't just me. When the five of us met it was not to pick over my infidelities but to debate how we were all going to face the new realities. We talked of how, even though we were all women in our thirties, it was still possible to say: "This just isn't good enough for me. I have to try something new." After these discussions I no longer felt so alone.

September and October are my favourite months in Ottawa. The turning leaves, the lack of mosquitoes, the annual Indian Summer melt me as nothing else does in the capital. My fantasies about settling in Vancouver had not survived a little rational thought, so I had returned to Stornoway. One afternoon I drove to pick up the boys from school. Dawdling down a tree-lined road I passed a little house with a "For Sale" sign on it: the words jolted me into action. *That* was what I would do: buy a house. And what's more buy one in Ottawa, to be near the boys so that they could spend weekends with me.

Now luck was on my side. Dropping the boys off at home, I hurried over to see my friend Rosemary and told her of my plans. She looked delighted: "Margaret, I have the perfect house for you. My friends the Lawries are selling a house they have spent the past four years renovating. It's perfect, and it's only just been put on the market."

I wanted to see the house immediately, but had to wait as the Lawries were on holiday in Maine. I could hardly contain my impatience. The day they returned I rushed over. It took no more than a minute for me to know that I had found my home. The house has an old-fashioned screen porch off the living room: that was enough. I stood gazing at it; there was no need to look further.

One other thing was going my way at last: money.

While Pierre continued to give me none, I was for the first time in my life in the process of earning large sums of money of my own. *Beyond Reason* was now an international best seller. The money flowed in, if not to me, then to the Marqusees at Paddington Press, and if they seemed to be taking their time about passing it on, I wasn't worried. The Lawries were asking a hundred and thirty-five thousand dollars; I offered a hundred and thirty-three because the living room had not been painted. They agreed. Overruling the protests of my lawyer since 1977, Morton (Cookie) Lazarus (he felt that I was neither rich nor rational enough to make such a decision), I cabled Paddington to send me my first installment of sixty thousand dollars. With some reluctance, they did. Then I signed my house contract.

My new home charmed me a little more every day. It stood on a very pretty street five minutes' drive from the official Ottawa of Stornoway and 24 Sussex, which made it wonderfully convenient for the boys. And when I had time to take it in, I found that what I had bought was attractive, unpretentious, superbly renovated. With track lighting, pine floors and white paint it was both modern and cozy. It needed very little doing to it, but what I did, I decided to do as beautifully and elegantly as I could. My first need was heavy curtains against the winter cold, but my priority was the main bedroom – my bedroom, the master bedroom and not an attic, the only room that was papered in something I disliked.

I had always dreamed of a pink bedroom. Now came the chance to fulfill my wish: I had the walls painted blush pink, laid a thick pale pink carpet and hung flowery, Japanese-looking curtains over the windows. (Only later was I told that pink is now known to be a soothing, womb-like colour, and that prison wardens have taken to painting sections of prisons pink for its calming effect on the inmates.)

Carpet and linen and china I brought up from the New

York apartment I had borrowed from friends and now returned to them. A bit more, such as bunks for the boys and kitchen equipment, I bought. Then another stroke of luck came my way. As I was about to get myself still deeper in debt and buy good furniture, the Faulkners offered me the loan of their large collection of antique furniture, as they were moving down to an already furnished country house outside Montreal.

The day the furniture arrived in November 1979, I finally understood what had happened to me: I had landed on my feet. Letting myself into the house with my key I danced round and round the bare kitchen, like a woman possessed, whirling with an intensity of happiness that I had forgotten I was capable of. The first caller at my new home was a large van from Johnson's Furniture delivering a butcher block kitchen table. I solemnly laid a picnic lunch out on it and proceeded to inaugurate my new life.

Pierre had not been to visit my new establishment but, watching my activities from the sidelines, had been spurred on to do a little house-hunting of his own. He had decided that he would retire, when the day came to leave politics, to French-speaking Montreal, so he now started searching the outskirts of the city for a suitable house. Typically, he settled on the only house in Montreal that has been designated an historical site, an art deco mansion on Pine Avenue designed in 1930 by Ernest Cormier, the Quebec architect who designed Ottawa's Supreme Court.

Sometime in late November I awakened to the sound of furious hammerings on my door. When I opened it I discovered the small front garden bathed in lights and thick with journalists and television crews.

"Hey Mrs Trudeau," called one reporter, "could you please give us your reaction?"

I was confused. Reaction to what? Luckily another

shouted out: "What do you feel about your husband's resignation as leader of the Liberal Party?"

I kept my head. "I have no intention at all of giving you my reaction," I said, as pleasantly as I could, and quickly shut the door again.

Then I stood there shaking, rage against Pierre building up. How could he do this to me? How could he make this sort of fundamental decision and not even tell me so that I looked a fool? I went upstairs, dressed, picked up the boys' cat, which had spent the night with me, and roared over to Stornoway to find out what was going on.

Pierre simply laughed at me. The more I stormed up and down, saying, "Why didn't you tell me? Did you think you couldn't trust me?" the more he laughed. I realized then that he saw it all as a game: he was trying to exclude me from his life, just as I was trying to exclude him from mine.

I wasn't wholly surprised about his decision though. All through the summer and early autumn of 1979 Pierre had become increasingly despondent about the powerlessness of an opposition leader. He felt, I think, that there was no real role for him in the political future of the country. And he was sixty-one. If he was to have any other sort of future himself, now was the time to begin it.

His resignation was greeted with consternation by the Liberals. Accolades to Pierre were heard from one end of Canada to the other, and once the news was out, all his old popularity returned. In newspaper articles and news bulletins writers and reporters sang the praises of a prime minister whom only lately they had been knocking. Now, they chose to remember his charisma, his incredible drive, his success at giving the country such an international aura. Pierre basked in remembered glory, even if he dismissed the paeans of praise as "my obituaries."

And then, scarcely three weeks later, Joe Clark's government decided to present a budget. In itself neither unusual nor unexpected, the budget turned out to be the greatest political fiasco of Joe Clark's career. To get it through, the Conservatives needed the support of the left-wing New Democratic Party, yet what they did was prepare a budget that on social and economic grounds was absolutely bound to be rejected by any even vaguely socialist party. Among others, Nancy Jamieson, Clark's legislative assistant, warned that it would spell disaster. No one listened. The night the Conservatives were defeated on the floor of the house, Joe Clark was compelled to call an election.

This put both Pierre and the Liberals in a quandary. Not only was there no obvious successor to Pierre in the party but, under Liberal rules, there was no time now before a general election to hold a leadership convention and pick one. Pierre deliberated; the Liberals deliberated. Within a couple of days the news came back: Pierre was not going to resign as leader. "It is my duty," he told reporters, "to accept the draft of the party." He vowed to fight like crazy to bring the Liberals back to power and once back he was not going to resign at once either, but carry right on with what he saw as his rightful job: that of Prime Minister. The reporters were dumbfounded. Some of the writers felt they had overdone the praise.

The challenge did a lot for Pierre. From despondent and depressed he became, overnight, a fighter once more and this time he fought a brilliant campaign. Defeat had humbled him, and for the time being at least he had lost his arrogant and sneering manner. He gave an excellent speech, making no promises beyond getting the country running efficiently again. Then he set off on a tour, not of the major cities, but of the smaller towns where he is most loved. Wherever he stopped the crowds came out to wish him luck.

As with the 1974 election, all now swung his way.

Seven months earlier Joe Clark had been able to sit back and pick up the anti-Trudeau vote; the roles were now reversed. Six months of a Conservative government under a man who spent his time either entertaining or listening to advice that invariably turned out to be wrong had convinced the Canadian people that they wanted once again a Prime Minister who knew his own mind, who did his homework, who worked sixteen hours a day not because he was a workaholic but because he believed that it was the duty of the Prime Minister to be one step ahead of everybody.

Poor Joe came out of it all very badly: it soon became a joke in Ottawa that all Joe had done during his time in office was change the parting in his hair, and that was only on the advice of a public relations firm that told him the people didn't trust him because he had such a funny haircut. As for Maureen, the election could not have come at a worse time: she was deep in her law exams and had to divide her time between her studies and frantic canvassing.

As for me, the timing of the election, the little quirk in Canada's political history, turned out to be a miracle of good fortune. For while Pierre turned his attentions to a serious campaign, I got the boys. And because of my house, and my evident new stability, even Pierre agreed that I was in a position to look after them. So when he left Stornoway to travel around the country the boys packed their bags, collected the cat and moved over to my place.

Now began a good period of my life – on the practical level, at least. Ten years of official residences and laundresses and cleaning ladies had not accustomed me to domestic chores and at first I found that my time was wholly given to washing and ironing jeans and scrubbing the kitchen table. For over a decade I had thrown my dirty clothes on the floor, only to find them back in my drawer, clean and pressed. Now, unless I did something about them, they lay turning into mould in the corner. Gradually, of course, I improved. What started as a fantasy, a make-believe playing at being mother and housewife, quickly turned into a routine. I thought it was the start of a normal life.

As it turned out, I was quite wrong. There were a lot of hiccoughs, many setbacks, before I was to find stability. The first of December brought the first of a series of shocks. My second cheque arrived from Paddington Press: I was relieved to get it, for by now I was much in debt over my extravagant curtains and carpets and the various things I had been unable to resist buying for the house. Two days after I had presented the cheque to my bank, I got a phone call. The cheque had bounced.

"Bounced?" I said to the manager with a laugh. "No, that's not possible. It is from a publishing company."

The manager's voice was grim. "I'm sorry Mrs Trudeau. We've been informed that all accounts belonging to Paddington Press have been closed."

I put the phone down. I still couldn't quite believe what was happening. The phone rang again: this time it was the lawyer who had arranged the book deal, Steve Martindale of Washington. Paddington Press had gone into receivership. It was quite simple: no more money.

The news was more disastrous than even I had realized. When I came to add up all I owed, the sum horrified me: an overdraft of sixty thousand dollars at the bank, a mortgage of seventy-five thousand dollars on the house, two thousand dollars a month in repayments alone. Then there were the bills for furniture and the curtains and carpets. My God, I thought, what *am* I going to do? How am I going to survive?

If it seems strange that I did not immediately turn to Pierre, there is one very simple explanation: I had embarked on all this against Pierre's wishes, and he had made it clear that I did so entirely at my own risk.

I did, of course, think hard about whether to go to my

parents for help, and in some small way I already had, since my mother had paid for most of my curtains. But it was more complicated than simply asking for help. A lifetime's pride was involved.

As soon as was possible, shortly after my seventeenth birthday, I had left my parents' home to go to university. Even at that age I didn't want to be dependent on them. For me to turn to them now would have been to admit defeat and, crushed as I was, I still intended to rely on my own resourcefulness. Had they realized the extent of my debts, I know they would have offered to send me money from Vancouver, but I had no intention of crawling to Daddy for help. His Scottishness and my own innate horror of sponging made that unthinkable.

Besides, I had two very good lessons to put steel in my heart. Once, in the early days of my marriage, I had gone to my father when bills from Creeds rose to over two thousand dollars, letters of demand were coming thick and fast and Pierre had flatly refused to pay them. Daddy sent the money, of course, but with it came a scorching letter of reproof, berating me for being an appalling spendthrift and questioning with considerable distaste what it was about me that made me spend money this way.

And as if this wasn't enough, I still retained a clear childhood memory of an old relative who kept falling on bad times and coming to my father for loans. He always got them, but he never managed to escape the contempt that his "scrounging," as my father blisteringly put it, led to. So I knew now, with absolute certainty, that anything I asked for would involve a brutal lecture – and that I could not face.

Then came the 1979 Christmas holidays. First Christmas itself: Pierre and I had agreed that I would sleep at Stornoway on the night of Christmas Eve, so as to be there when the children awakened on Christmas morning. I had used my Visa charge card to buy presents, having run completely out of cash and not daring to approach the bank for more. I arrived to find the floor strewn with presents and the tree already decorated. That stabbed my heart, because decorating the tree has always been an obsession with me, but the occasion promised well enough.

My satisfaction was short-lived. For one thing the wrapped parcels for the boys contained, not personal presents but handouts gathered by Pierre at ceremonies of one kind or another – models of tractors from tractor factories – and given to the nanny to wrap. For another, there was nothing, not one single present, for me, and I found that this first, poignant exclusion was horribly painful.

Before lunch, Pierre, the three boys and I returned to my house, for my tree and my gifts. It was not a merry day. The boys seemed to sense that this was my territory and even they resented Pierre's intrusion. After lunch, I told him about Paddington Press. By now my lawyers had filed a claim in bankruptcy court but I was well aware that their legal costs were building up and had been warned that if John Marqusee could delay the case by technicalities he would do so to give himself time to dissolve his assets. Once that was done, I thought there was less hope of money. Pierre was not sympathetic. Perhaps it was too much to hope, given his ambivalence about *Beyond Reason*. You've brought this on yourself, he seemed to be saying.

Pierre was due to sign the papers for his new house on New Year's Eve and asked me to take the boys down to meet him in Montreal so that they could see it. I arranged to stay with the Faulkners while he took Justin and Sacha to a hockey game. Then we would inspect the house together.

I had seen it myself earlier in the autumn and been somewhat distressed by the notion of it as a family home. Cormier's extravaganza had been on the market for twenty years: a great bunker-like building, more mausoleum than home, it dominated the side of a hill, the two levels that made it up seeming to cascade from one to the other. The problem was that it had two master suites, well divided from each other, but nothing suitable for small boys. Pierre's assurance to me that he would split these up in such a way that each child had his own patch had not really reassured me. It seemed a bleak sort of place, soundproof and lightless, full of chilly marble floors in ornate geometric patterns. The contrast between our two choices of home, Pierre's and mine, was vastly revealing of a difference in taste and character so profound that it made me wonder how we had ever managed together at all. I couldn't imagine how the boys would react to their future home with any pleasure.

I was wrong. I hadn't reckoned on the water bed. Down in the bottom suite stood a magnificent water bed and this they fell onto with exclamations of incredulity. So excited were they that they charged about the glassy marble floors with whoops of pleasure.

"At last, like you, I know the joys of owning a house," Pierre said to me jovially over a glass of champagne. Ah yes, I reflected bitterly. For three hundred thousand dollars. It must be nice.

That night, having toasted Pierre and his election campaign, having inspected his future and found it prosperous, we returned to Ottawa. Pierre came into the house to help me put the boys to bed. As he was about to leave I asked him for some money. I tried to sound reasonable. "Perhaps Pierre, since you will be campaigning for the next couple of months and the boys will be living here, you might give me some sort of allowance for their keep?" was how I put it.

Pierre reached casually into his pocket and took out his wallet. "I don't think I've got much on me, Margaret. Will fifty dollars do?" His narrow eyes and slightly sneering laugh seemed to mock me.

Something burst inside me. A three-hundred-thousand-dollar house and all he was proposing was fifty dollars. It wasn't just mean, it was humiliating. He knew my debts. What did he think I was going to do?

I don't remember much after that. I know I went for his eyes with my nails and had every intention of blinding him first and killing him afterward. I know that at that instant I hated him with a purer hate than I knew I possessed.

Within seconds I found myself pinned down by his arms on the ground: Pierre is a brown belt in judo and had little trouble protecting himself. But I kept screaming, the sound coming from my mouth in bursts. The children awakened and stood, shocked, observing us.

"Daddy don't hurt Mummy, don't hurt Mummy," Sacha kept pleading.

Pierre shook me: "Be quiet, Margaret, pull yourself together."

I kept yelling.

In time, the rage passed, but it was really Micha who saved the day. As Pierre and I were sitting weakly in the bedroom, Micha called to Pierre to come to his room. They were gone half an hour, talking things over and Pierre always says that Micha put a lot of sense into him. Then he left. We were both shaken. I felt deeply ashamed, haunted by the boys' looks of mesmerized fear. And I was deeply confused.

I think that day I reached my emotional bottom. Reviewing my life once more I could see only questions and all were unanswerable. Without money, with no obvious source of income other than the charity of my parents, how were we going to live? Without a man, without the affection I craved, what was my future to be? With my friends all leaving Ottawa, to whom could I turn? Without my family's moral support, how was I going to bring up the boys? Without hope, in fact, how was I going to survive?

Chapter Nine
On Being Mad

No account of my past few years would be complete without reference to what the public, Pierre, my family and most of my friends believed to be my "mental breakdowns" and "cures." I myself never seriously believed, deep down inside, that I was mad. That instinct for survival probably saved me. But it is certainly true that as I grew more confused it was increasingly hard not to be convinced by the certainty of those around me. Very often, alone and frightened, I came close to believing in my own insanity.

The story of my mental depression starts long before the timespan covered in this book. If I only touched on it in *Beyond Reason*, it was because I was still living it and the events and feelings were too raw for me to describe without considerable pain. For the sake of clarity I shall begin where the doubts began, and gather into this one chapter all the steps, wherever they fall chronologically, in this unhappy and, I now know, profoundly misinterpreted saga.

The first time in my life it occurred to me to question my sanity was after the 1974 election campaign. Those two months of intense hard work, both alongside Pierre and off on my own, talking at political rallies up and down Canada, submerging my interests in the needs of someone else, being welcomed by the Liberal campaigners as part of a working team, had been a revelation to me. Even if I only formulated it more clearly later, what that time taught me was that as long as I could have a role in Pierre's life, an honest, demanding job of my own, then I would survive. Serving tea to visiting diplomats had not been enough: this first glimpse of the real world of political strife was a very different matter.

The trouble was that the very nature of the event made my part ephemeral: I ended the campaign as I began it, as Pierre's wife. We wound up the campaign on a brilliant blue day in Toronto, the political touchstone of the country and thus vital to Pierre's success. Exhaustion, hope, determination all combined to make me give the best speech of my life to one hundred and fifty thousand people assembled with their picnics on Toronto Island. I talked to them about children and families and motherhood; the listening crowd seemed moved; a few had tears on their cheeks. I felt moved myself. Pierre had spoken before me, to rapturous applause. Others spoke after. The atmosphere radiated success.

That night Pierre and I flew back to Ottawa. It was there the following evening that we heard of our stupendous victory. The next morning dawned blue and sunny. I took my breakfast out onto the porch behind 24 Sussex and sat watching the white sails on the glistening river below me, while I waited to be praised for the part I had played in the campaign. No praise came. I waited for Pierre to come to me to discuss what sort of political future I might have beside him. He never came.

It was then that I felt used, manipulated by the whole political machine and cast aside. I felt tricked, as if someone had gone to great lengths to build me up, only to mock me afterward for my temerity in daring to believe in myself. The point was: I felt involved. I had acquired confidence in my own political acumen, in my ability to judge the mood of crowds, the expectations of strangers.

136

I believed the moment had perhaps come for me to enter the political arena, not as part of the coffee and sandwiches brigade but as a member of the decision-making process, the inner circle of the party, even if only in press or public relations. It wasn't that I had worked out exactly what I wanted, beyond a vague notion that I might become the sort of political companion to Pierre that Rosalynn Carter later became to Jimmy. But that morning, sitting drinking my coffee, I fully expected that Pierre and his colleagues had seen my worth.

I also felt somewhat confused. The public speaking, the cheering audiences, the all-involving teamwork of the previous months, had given me a sudden and unnerving sense of my own power and with that came a horrible feeling of guilt. As a hippie and a flower child I had, along with my contemporaries, rejected ambitious and powerful people, despising from the bottom of my heart the kind of clawing ambition to get to the top that I could see around me among my father's colleagues.

And now suddenly here I was, highly conscious of the size of the audiences that came to listen to me, enjoying greatly the power that I seemed to have over them. My pleasure in this sort of manipulation – that's what made me guilty. I felt torn between a furtive revelling in my own charisma and a disgust that I should feel that way since the success was really Pierre's.

The sheer hard work of the previous months also had provided a diversion from doubts about my relationship with Pierre. Now sitting back at 24 Sussex, twenty-five years old, with a future so void of plan and hope that I could not believe in it, all the long-suppressed anxieties and uncertainties returned about whether Pierre and I were really at all compatible. With them came a fierce resentment against Pierre.

I felt he had used me worst of all, because he now seemed to go to cruel lengths to convey to me how deeply unimportant I was, how any importance I might ever acquire would only be as a function of my role as his wife. He ignored me. He didn't thank me for what I had done. He didn't acknowledge my success with the young. He never told me that I had done a good job. Like many men, he simply took the entire credit himself for the Liberal victory. Whenever I tried to talk politics he brushed me off. He was tired, he said. He wanted to rest. He certainly didn't want to waste any time discussing his new cabinet or his strong majority with me. He just wanted to get me back into my place – at home with the children.

I resented, too, the way I had been forced into weaning Sacha too suddenly during the election campaign. Sacha was born on Christmas Day 1973. Pierre and I set off in May, taking him with us, since I was still breast-feeding him. He was a splendid campaigner, giving no trouble, and I would cheerfully have gone on nursing him until the end, had my mother and the friends we encountered as we journeyed across Canada not implored me to stop, telling me that I looked exhausted and that the constant travelling could only be harmful for such a small baby. Foolishly I had listened to them, and when Sacha was six months old I had handed him over to a close friend in Vancouver. The appalling idea that he might have felt rejected now began to haunt me.

The weeks following the Liberal victory were miserable ones for me. The campaign had been exhausting for everyone and all had gone off on well-deserved summer holidays with their families. When they returned to Ottawa three weeks later to take up government again, they had totally forgotten who I was. In any case, by then I felt broken down, tormented by doubts about Pierre, bitter about being so rejected, inadequate as a mother, and totally horrified by thoughts of the future.

My reaction was to take flight. Leaving Pierre and his

indifference, colleagues I now considered mediocre and ungrateful, and a stuffy official life whose crippling limitations I had kidded myself did not matter and now remembered did, I bought an airline ticket to Paris. I flew there on my own, then decided to go on to Greece. My rebellion had begun.

I had no definite plans, merely a desire to be on my own, so I made a sentimental pilgrimage to the village where my childhood love, Yves Lewis, had been at school, and from there moved on to Crete, where I rented a car, swam, took photographs. I carried about with me only a blanket to sleep under and a small knapsack with a change of clothes. I smoked a lot of cannabis. I idled the days away in adolescent reveries. And I pushed firmly to the back of my consciousness a terrifying feeling that was beginning to overpower me that there was something wrong with my mind, that all my doubt and fear and bitterness were being caused, not by outside factors, but by something medically wrong with me. Hadn't my father questioned my sanity after all my wild spending? Hadn't other wives been through political campaigns, just as intensely as I had, but then emerged tranquil and secure?

At this point in my life, abruptly, my emotional future opened up, as if I had suddenly changed gears. I returned from Crete in time to accompany Pierre to the Robert Kennedy celebrity pro tennis tournament in New York and it was there that I fell in love with my charming senator. Looking back on it, the passion I felt for this delightful man was clearly not love. It was need, need for recognition and affection.

Back in Canada, provoked by Pierre's hostility and coldness, I told him that I had fallen in love. His reaction was characteristic. "You're sick," he said at once. "You're mad. If you weren't mad, you wouldn't do this." He stormed and then froze me out. "You need professional help." Only many years later did it occur to me that someone who equates falling in love with insanity is not himself a model of mental stability.

But I believed him. I followed his instructions meekly and checked into Montreal's Royal Victoria Hospital to be made sane again. The trouble was that I yearned for the company of fellow patients in the psychiatric wing, but found myself instead in an executive suite usually reserved for aging businessmen and their prostate operations, attended by a psychiatrist who seemed always to be wiping gravy from his fat, greasy face.

Too confused and guilty to protest, I acquiesced in a treatment of mind-numbing drugs that left me comatose on my bed, hardly able to listen to an endlessly blaring television, too dopey and nauseous to protest, so subservient I didn't even want to. What I did want to do was talk. I was already bored. But the Thorazine they gave me made my tongue swell up.

I might have stayed there for months had it not been for the hospital priest. Unlike the psychiatrists, who scorned my attempts to talk, to explain and to try to understand despite the Thorazine-induced lethargy, the priest was very ready to listen to me, and wonderfully ready to support me. He seemed to understand that what I needed was real life, not this mausoleum of the senses. It was only when he started questioning me sternly about having simply abandoned my children and given up that I found I had the strength to store the pills I was given under my tongue and throw them down the toilet when the nurses left the room.

It was then that I started doing a little serious thinking of my own. Pierre, I deliberated, was not interested in my mind, or my personality, or my maturation. What he wanted was a decorative child-making machine, a plastic wife to rear his children and decorate his home, a symbol, not a person. He despised me at heart as an uncultured, unsophisticated Western Canadian. His own background prevented him from understanding weakness. Intolerant by nature, his Jesuit training had made him subjugate all matters of the heart to the strictures of the mind. From this stemmed a natural way of thinking: I had fallen in love, quite simply, not out of wickedness – how could any wife of Pierre be wicked? – but out of madness. Because to fall in love on purpose would be like cheating on your Harvard exams, too despicable to be contemplated.

Pierre, I realized for the first time, in a blinding flash of perception, was neither generous nor compassionate. If I was going to stay with him, I would have to accept that. Now, at a distance of many years, I know that the fact that I could not accept him as he was provoked our frequent fights and the eventual breakdown of our marriage.

As the days went by I kept asking the doctors and nurses who visited me: "Am I crazy? Please tell me. Do you think I'm crazy?"

"No, of course not," they all replied soothingly. "You just need a little rest. You need to calm down, get away from your problems, take it easy."

One day the doctor asked me to write my own report on myself. In it I explained in detail what I saw to be Pierre's lack of generosity and compassion and how this seemed to affect me. I gave specific examples of the ways in which he had humiliated me over money. The doctor found it hard to conceal his astonishment at my lucidity. It was the first time I saw him start to question the assumption held by all the doctors who came to see me that there was actually something wrong with my mind.

No diagnosis was ever made. Opinions dissolved into woolly medical jargon that meant nothing. I discharged myself from hospital, gaunt but determined.

That I was no better – since all continued to see my

condition as medical and therefore "curable" – was apparent, I later learned, to all the friends who came to visit me when I got home. I was still sad, confused and angry. That was the problem. I lived my so-called disease on many different levels, all of them false. There was my hatred of official life. There was my unrecognized passion for my American senator, which sparked once more and turned into a brief and wonderful affaire, only to fade and die. There was my unhappy relationship with Pierre, who seemed glad to have me home but, angry about my affaire, refused to discuss anything. He preferred to see me as a broken down car sent to the mechanic and now returned to him in less than working order.

Pierre talked to some colleagues about my problems, then sent me to see a psychiatrist in Ottawa twice a week for about six weeks. The doctor and I, it soon became clear, had very different notions about psychiatry. He wouldn't make a diagnosis, though he did say that he didn't think it could have anything to do with postnatal depression, as the Montreal psychiatrist at one point suggested. All he would say was that he was going to get me "back to being a very happily married woman."

He wanted me to conform so that I would be able to lead the life expected of me. I wanted to know who the hell I was. We might have been speaking different languages. When I told him that I smoked a lot of pot simply to help me to cope, he didn't think it was a problem. He thought it was silly and must be given up and could, of course, be given up at a moment's notice. He didn't realize how psychologically necessary it had become to me, a foil to Pierre's rigid priestly attitude, a counterbalance to his intellectual purity.

There was no future for that psychiatrist and me, a point I demonstrated with blinding clarity the day I rolled myself the biggest joint I had ever smoked, arrived almost too high to make sense and talked at him for an hour, only to be told that I was now well on the way to recovery since I could speak so freely with no help from drugs. "Huh to you," I said, and left his office for good.

The next three years I did without psychiatric help. I was not tempted to look for it. I preferred to sit and chat with my friends, Nancy, Jane, Gro and Rosemary, about the vicissitudes of daily living, or go out for lunch with men who made me laugh. Unlike the rest of the world, which seemed to accept that I was prone to "mental problems," that I was flighty and fickle and suffered from "emotional distress," I was now beginning to suspect that the disorder lay, not inside me alone, but inside my marriage. Pierre was bent on punishing me. For weeks on end he refused to make love to me. Our marriage seeped quietly away. Looking back on it, I know that if only I had summoned up the confidence to pursue my convictions and to face Pierre squarely we would have been spared much unhappiness. As it was, almost six years were to pass before I was to be cleared of all taints of "madness."

I did, though, think of one other source of help. I had become a Catholic when I married Pierre. I had grown to love the rituals of the church and to feel close to God, if not to His ministers. After my talks to the hospital priest in Montreal I tried to read books of religious inspiration. But as my marriage got worse, and the world came to see in me the original scarlet woman, so these texts lost all power to soothe me.

My next encounter with the psychiatric profession took place in New York. By 1977 I was making frequent visits to the U.S., where I stayed with friends and tried to pursue some career of my own for the brief spells of time I was by then living away from Pierre. It was on one of these visits my friend Yasmin Aga Khan suddenly said to me: "Look, I can't go on listening to all this. Don't you realize what Pierre is doing to you? Don't you under-

143

stand that you have no self-esteem, no self-respect and that's what is making you behave so wildly? You're becoming just what Pierre says you are: destructive and willful and irrational. It's like a self-fulfilling prophecy. Soon you *will* be mad."

It was through Yasmin that I started going to Dr Arnold Hutchnecker, and I believe now that it was this remarkable, cultured, eighty-year-old Freudian – the analyst everyone dreams of – who started me on my road to recovery. Dr Hutchnecker was expensive, seventy-five dollars an hour, and I went to him twice a week. He knew what interested him: people who deal in power and how it affects them. But he was also human, a gentle Viennese, and he seemed to understand what was wrong with me.

And so, two afternoons a week, on and off for over six months, I made my way to his office on Park Avenue and talked. It was a deeply soothing room, with a Renoir hanging over his mahogany desk, thick carpets and soft colours, a timeless, reassuring place.

Dr Hutchnecker talked too. He told me that I was being very masochistic in simply accepting Pierre's coldness and his meanness over money, and that passivity of that kind merely made other people more sadistic. He said that he believed I was right to leave, before I lost all love of life and spontaneity. He was quite firm with me. Did I really want to become the sort of martyr everyone exploits? Did I actually like being so plaintive?

It was Dr Hutchnecker who first gave a name to the sense of anguish and impotence I had bottled up inside me: "inner rage," he called it, a fury I had been suppressing for too long against a man who dominated me and a world I felt oppressed me. He added that in his opinion this state of agitation now lay under the thinnest veneer of conformity and tolerance and that I must take steps to prevent it from erupting in neurotic and irrational behav-

144

iour. "To live properly," he said, "you must learn to bring that inner rage to the surface. You must take up acting, you must express yourself, you must indulge your senses. You must fight to participate in life, not feel cowed by it."

Often, we talked about my father and Pierre. As a child, I felt constantly neglected by my father. Dr Hutchnecker now made me see that much of my attitude toward Pierre was based on a desire to please him as a daughter rather than as a wife, that I had looked in our marriage for the perfect father, and found instead a stern companion. He showed me that I was too hard on Pierre, that it was wrong to demand of him things he could not give me, like omniscient approval and forgiveness. Instead, I should accept his weaknesses and love him for his own qualities.

To my surprise and intense relief, Dr Hutchnecker was totally uncensorious about drugs. First cautiously, then as I saw how calm he remained, with total honesty, I related to him my many years of experimentation with different drugs, my periods of dependence on the relaxing effects of marijuana, my ups and downs with cocaine. Dr Hutchnecker listened carefully, questioned me closely. He warned me to remain wary of all artificially induced emotions, but he did not criticize.

It was this permissiveness that made it possible for me to do without drugs. I knew they were there. Dr Hutchnecker had somehow reassured me that they were not sinful. So I felt able for the first time in years to put them aside, and though I was to return to them, with terrible effects, his words remained with me, and later made it possible for me to assess what harm they did me.

After about five months of these sessions I realized that I was fast running out of money and that Dr Hutchnecker was becoming a luxury I could ill afford. Reluctant to let go of a helping hand I knew was guiding me

145

closer by the week to mental strength, I approached Pierre for at least a contribution to the fees. He refused. So the day came when I had to go to my Viennese friend and tell him that my last session had come.

Dr Hutchnecker listened carefully, then told me to return once again. On what I took to be my final visit he suddenly said: "I have been thinking. Psychiatry is not a business. It's a service. I'm your lifeline, and I have come to believe that I am really helping you come to terms with problems that I know to be serious. I am sure that one day you will be on your own feet. Pay me then."

And so the sessions went on. But not for long. The invitation to make *Kings and Desperate Men* came my way, and I was in New York less and less. In any case, by then Dr Hutchnecker had done something that was nothing short of miraculous for me: like a good fairy in a children's tale, he had returned to me the beginnings of my self-respect. My recovery had begun, though I still had many setbacks in store. And when, not long after, I got paid, I used my first installments to return Dr Hutchnecker's generosity.

The beginning of my growth toward independence did not, however, make for closer relations with Pierre. In fact, as I grew in mental distance from him, so our relationship worsened. A glimmer of understanding about myself and the complex machinery of the mind had given me for the first time some kind of ammunition with which to confront Pierre. Instead of spluttering rage I now had sensible, rational words with which to back up my fury, learned words of psychology, psychiatry and psychoanalysis. This only served to madden him more. He didn't want a partner who seemed to know better than he did. And so our arguments grew more vicious, each of us armed with knowledge and an intent to inflict pain.

Later, a Canadian named Linda Griffiths co-wrote and

146

starred in a play based on my life with Pierre. She collected the material for the script by posing as a drama student and interviewing anyone willing to talk who knew us at all. What she came up with was an outstandingly perceptive play, called *Maggie & Pierre*, in which she does a remarkable job of playing all three roles: Maggie, Pierre, and a journalist named Henry. When I saw the play in Vancouver, there was one scene that struck me as deadly accurate.

Maggie is leaving Pierre and begging him to come with her, and of course he won't, being obsessed by his power and importance as a politician. Henry, the journalist, is listening to Pierre (that's where the play was wrong, Pierre would never talk like that to a journalist), who is saying:

You know something, Henry? As we were going through all those horrendous fights, my wife was at my feet, and she was crying and screaming and wailing and literally banging her head against the wall, and I stood there, frozen, in the classic pose of man, locked in my own gender, not knowing whether to go to her and comfort her, or leave because it's too personal to watch, or hit her, or what to do. And my dominant emotion was jealousy. . . that she could be so free. . . . ©

When I heard those lines my immediate reaction was: that's *exactly* how it was. Indeed, Linda Griffiths got it right. Pierre never once, in our marriage, acted to save me. He wanted me prostrate, at his feet. In personal relationships he's a taker, not a giver. I came to see how over the years I had shared everything with him, my dreams, my thoughts, but he had never reciprocated properly, never allowed himself to be exposed.

The next and worst phase of my supposed insanity was still to come. It started in August 1979, the month that Celest Fremon chose to destroy me in *Playgirl*. Her revelations – of my abortion at seventeen, my various affaires, my drug-taking – were all the proof that Pierre needed that I was truly mad. And this time, when he shouted at me once again: "You're sick. Don't you see, you're mad. How could you behave this way if you weren't?" I believed him.

My poor mother only made matters worse. A CBC reporter got her on the phone one day and I heard her say, in answer to some question I could not hear: "Well, I suppose she *must* be crazy." She meant nothing but well. She was desperately worried, harried by the reporters who kept phoning, and she clearly hadn't stopped to think. Instead of confronting her with it, I brooded. So she doubts my sanity too, I kept thinking.

It was at this point that a Liberal politician decided to intervene in my mental affairs, in the shape of Stuart Smith, then leader of the Ontario Liberal Party. Stuart is young, intelligent, a good politician and, as it happens, a psychiatrist. Sometime late in the summer of 1979, after the *Playgirl* article, he phoned Pierre – more out of concern for the Liberal Party's standing than my wellbeing I have no doubt – and tentatively suggested that I might be suffering from manic depression.

"This is not a proper diagnosis," he said to Pierre. "It's just that I have been following the press reports and from the various accounts of your wife's moods, the way they go up, then fall to lows of depression, it just occurred to me that she might be manic depressive."

The first I knew of this conversation was when Pierre asked me casually a couple of days later whether I had ever considered the possibility of some more serious disorder. Did I know, he went on, that there was now a treatment for manic depression, called lithium, that was

meant to stabilize moods? At this stage in our relationship my guilt was such that I would have agreed to
anything.

Stuart Smith came to Ottawa to see me. No one
wanted to make this public, and in any case he was no
longer practising as a psychiatrist, so we met at Jane
Faulkner's house. Though our meeting was hardly conclusive, I remember it in detail.

It was a brilliant, sunny September day and we sat
inside, in the living room. Our conversation lasted about
three hours as Dr Smith, with his thin wire glasses and
nervous manner, tried hard to mould me into what was
clearly a strongly held preconceived notion about my
mind. Did I often feel sad? When did I feel sad? For how
long? Did my sadness then give way to bouts of
euphoria, impulsiveness, sleeplessness? How long did
my happy moments last? And so on.

I answered him to the best of my ability. I told him that
I was indeed very sad, very guilty about what I had done
to Pierre and the Canadian public, very humiliated about
people's responses to me. I told him the only time I was
not sad was when I was with my children or friends.

I'm not sure how hard he listened. Certainly he didn't
bother to follow up on my remarks about drug-taking
and never inquired about cocaine. At that stage I still
hadn't realized just what the drugs did to me – and
neither had Dr Smith. Finally, seemingly at a slight loss,
he recommended a psychiatrist friend in Toronto and
slipped away down Jane's garden path as furtively as he
had come.

Obediently, I took a plane to Toronto for a meeting
with Dr Kingstone. It was a beautiful autumn day and,
sitting in a friend's garden in the sunshine, feeling for a
moment happy and relaxed, I could not help reflecting
somewhat bitterly that all these attempts to make me out
as mad were beside the point.

Even Dr Kingstone had his doubts. He told me that manic depression is cyclical and he too asked hopefully if I suffered bouts of euphoria followed by lows of depression. "No," I replied firmly, by now bored with this line of questioning. "I don't. I feel humiliated, hurt by life, tremendously sad and a victim, but I do not go up and down in my emotions."

Dr Kingstone appeared still more doubtful. Finally, with some reluctance, he said: "Well, it is quite possible you're manic depressive...we'd better put you on lithium. Then if the diagnosis is right, you'll feel much, much better. And if you're not, then all the drug will do to you is make you feel a little less creative."

That should have warned me. But I made just one feeble protest.

"Less creative? How exactly? Must I take these pills?"

Any reluctance I felt was quickly dispelled by members of my family, who gathered around to impress on me the importance of giving my "cure" a try.

I took my first lithium in the early autumn of 1979, not long before buying my home. For the first few months I had to have a blood test each week to check that the dosage was right, because lithium is not a chemical, but an organic salt, and is highly toxic if taken out of proportion to the amount the body can absorb.

But soon, the "right" dose reached, I was on my own, out in solitary limbo where no one could, or as it seemed to me in my mildly paranoid state, wanted to, contact me. I soon sank to a level of consciousness more like hibernation than life. I was barely able to look after the children and do rudimentary housework.

Sometimes I thought, through the fog of my mind, that the boys were probably enjoying their gentle, quiet mother. Once they had left for school in the morning, I went back to bed and fell into a deep and dreamless sleep until their return. Once they were in bed at night, I returned again to the pink decorated bedroom I had designed for myself with such loving care, to a mindless addiction to television and to yet more sleep. As the days went by and lithium seemed to invade my system, I sank further into torpor and a troubling form of dizziness. Bed was the only place I felt safe.

But I was also hungry, agonizingly, persistently hungry, and so I would drag myself from my pillow, phone the local store to deliver the groceries, devour hamburgers, Cokes, pasta, crumpets, toast and jam, and then stagger back to bed. I gave up reading. I also gave up movies, theatre, conversation, friends and the outside world, in every shape and form.

No one seemed to notice. Of my close friends, only Rosemary was left in Ottawa and I kept her at a distance by telling her I had flu. Nancy, Gro and Jane had by now all left for their new lives.

By December a lingering part of myself, somewhere deep in my unconscious, grew anxious about this resigned descent into oblivion. Consulting a New York friend I learned of a lithium expert at Columbia University, a man whom I had met socially on Long Island and much admired. Summoning every last shred of energy, I caught the plane to New York to consult him. It was pouring rain. I took a cab to his clinic, which is part of the university medical school and situated far up in Harlem.

Before I saw the psychiatrist I had to fill out dozens of forms and questionnaires: about my patterns of sleep, my feelings, my sense of aggression, my sexual activities, my temper, my dreams. They seemed to go on forever. Then a nurse took some blood samples. Finally I was let in to see the doctor.

This session turned out to be no more conclusive or reassuring than any that had preceded it. The doctor looked at my forms, asked me a few more questions, then advised me to stick to the lithium since, he said, it was still too early to tell exactly what the drug could do for me. Since I complained of feeling debilitated and low, he suggested an antidepressant called Tofranil, one pill four times a day. This, he assured me, would make me less lethargic. At the same time he told me that he would like to see me again before too long. I departed to catch my plane for Ottawa.

Tofranil, which I now started taking in addition to the lithium, only served to make me nauseous, but that didn't stop me from eating. I developed a constant craving for I knew not what, a sort of inner starvation which I tried to feed by constantly gorging despite the psychiatrist's warning about going on a diet. After these daily orgies I felt sicker than ever. One day I tried shopping in a department store and passed out clean against a counter. After that I stayed at home.

By this time I had put on twenty-five pounds and still I was growing fatter. I had no lovers, no visitors and kept thinking of Jack Nicholson in *One Flew Over the Cuckoo's Nest*. The lithium, it seemed to me, was nothing other than an organic lobotomy: instead of removing aggression with the scalpel, it cut out all highs and lows with an infusion of poison.

Somewhere in the lighter recesses of my mind, however, I knew this could not go on. Occasionally I cut my dose down. Within days my head cleared, but at the same time I was beset by the most appalling withdrawal symptoms and so, reluctantly, I would return to my old dose. After all, it was cushioning me. I know now that a real crisis might have been precipitated when Paddington Press went into receivership had it not been for the fact that I could not really feel anything very deeply any more. When I heard of it, I sensed, rather than felt, the disaster. The caring had gone away.

And of course the few people I saw were reassured by my docility. This fat, placid, broken mare gave no trouble. Pierre was away campaigning all week and on weekends took the children off to Harrington Lake, while I put in a solid forty-eight hours' sleep. My family, during the autumn months, was in Vancouver. And no doctor came near me. I had two at this point, one in Toronto and one in Ottawa, and when I cancelled all their appointments, as I invariably did, each must have reassured himself that at least I was seeing the other.

The only person who watched what was happening and worried was Rosemary, who asked me over to her house constantly, and yet even she felt reluctant to intervene. Not hearing from me for days on end, she would come over to my house, find me dozing in bed, and say, "Margaret, this can't be right."

But when I seemed so contented, what was she to do? She kept reminding me of all the plans I had made for my new house: the new curtains I was going to make, the garden I had planned, the courses I was going to take. Paddington Press, I told her, had put an end to them. Besides, I couldn't see the point any more.

As Christmas approached, however, I began to realize that, on my own, I would never get around to buying presents for the boys or arranging for Christmas dinner. Heather Gillin came over one day to take me Christmas shopping. She was clearly appalled by what she saw. "You must go and phone your mother and tell her you need help," she instructed me firmly as she dropped me off at the door.

I called Vancouver. "Mum," I said weakly, "I don't think I can manage without you. Could you come?"

"Certainly, dear," she replied calmly, "I'll be there as soon as I can."

Two days later she arrived. Saying nothing, she set about making cookies, ordering a tree, buying presents, finding a turkey and shepherding the boys through Christmas activities. By Christmas Eve everything was in order and she departed again for Vancouver, leaving me prepared, if not exactly festive. That was the Christmas of my final bustup with Pierre.

This state of affairs might have gone on indefinitely had it not been for a Japanese promoter. One day early in the new year my phone in Ottawa rang. I answered it with reluctance, considering it another intrusion into my mindless reveries. It was Cookie Lazarus, my lawyer, telling me that a Japanese nightclub owner wanted me to come to Tokyo and open a new club for him. I listened, idly. A nightclub? And me so fat?

But then came something that jolted me into wakefulness. My Japanese admirer was offering twenty thousand dollars for the job. That was real money. I certainly needed it.

I don't know where I found the strength and determination to come off lithium and Tofranil. I do know that it was the hardest thing that I have ever done, and I can only compare what I went through with the accounts I have read of how heroin addicts feel when they come off dope. I woke up one morning and threw away all remaining pills. Once again I told Rosemary I had flu. Pierre, suspecting nothing, took the children off to Harrington Lake: he was back in Ottawa and it was his turn to have them. Then I closed the door and retired to my pink room.

For ten days I rarely left it. I sweated constantly; I threw up; I had diarrhea; I shook, first with cold, then with heat. I felt dizzy, weak, paranoid.

And then one morning I woke up feeling better; the poison was leaving my blood. I looked in the mirror and saw a fat mottled lump, but at least it was a lump with some sort of intelligence in her eyes. Enough to go on a fierce diet, dig out my good clothes and let them out, call Pierre and discuss the Japanese trip with him, and talk to Cookie about money. Enough to come to one startling,

154

crucial conclusion: the ups and downs the doctors had so lovingly examined were actually nothing more than my reaction to cocaine, the ups being when I took it, the downs when I took Valium to come off it. Drug abuse, not mental instability, had been the cause of my major symptoms all along.

That was my last experience of psychiatric medicine. From that day to this I have taken no miracle drug, consulted no psychiatrist or analyst. I should add something. None of the doctors I consulted ever called to find out what had become of me, to ask about my tolerance to lithium or even to check on my health. Pierre said nothing for a year and then, believing I was still on lithium, congratulated himself for having discovered the right "cure" for my mental condition. Even my mother never really questioned me closely. I rediscovered my own sanity, on my own, without help. For someone in my condition, psychiatry as I experienced it (not the psychoanalysis of Dr Hutchnecker, which probably saved my reason), is no more than a gigantic illusion.

Chapter Ten
Back On My Feet

I left for Japan on March 4, 1980, my ninth wedding anniversary. Before signing the deal I had asked Cookie to make certain that the offer was aboveboard. He came back from his enquiries enthusiastic. Nothing shady here. Dr Kichinosuke Sasaki, he confirmed, was a retired Japanese doctor who was going to invest his hard-earned money in a club. He would pay me an advance of four thousand dollars if I signed an agreement to fly to Tokyo for a week and make three half-hour personal appearances at his discothèque. The rest of the money would be waiting for me on my arrival. "The Japanese know how much you love their country," he reported Dr Sasaki as saying, "and they think of you as one of the foremost spokeswomen of your generation." It was hard to resist. Who would not be flattered by such words? Besides, I saw it as a chance for recovery.

But then reporters heard of the invitation and my trip nearly foundered. Pierre was at the height of his election campaign and the question raised again and again in the press was why a Japanese entrepreneur was choosing the wife of a past and not yet re-elected prime minister to visit his country. Was it official, or was it not? None of this was made easier when Dr Sasaki chose to give a very unfortunate interview in Tokyo. Questioned closely by foreign journalists as to why he was inviting me when victory for the Liberals was far from certain, he replied that he, for one, was sure that Pierre would win. But then he added: "In any case, she can't back out now, I've got her, she's signed a contract and I'll really make her pay for it if she pulls out. I mean, she's really in trouble if she doesn't come. I've got her, and I know everyone has a price."

These clumsy words maddened me, even if I didn't quite believe the newspapers to be reporting them right. I asked Pierre if he would look into the deal for me, and so he made a few discreet enquiries of his own, and came back with the news that he, like Cookie, could find nothing sinister in the offer.

"What *shall* I do?" I begged Pierre.

His reply was predictable: "You must do exactly what you want to do. You're your own best judge. It's fine by me."

Then he made a suggestion that had been lying dormant in my own mind. Just in case there was anything scandalous awaiting me, it might be a good idea to take a chaperone, in the form of my sister Janet, who was the perfect companion anyway because of her charm and easy manners. This seemed the ideal solution.

When I sent in my request to Dr Sasaki, there were no protests. First-class tickets were made out for both of us. But even the Japanese ambassador in Ottawa, whom I had tea with when I went to pick up our visas, was somewhat astonished by Dr Sasaki's extreme generosity.

Like everyone else, he pressed me: "What exactly are you going to *do*, Madame Trudeau?"

What indeed? I was far from certain myself.

From the first, my visit to Japan seemed charmed. Nothing had been neglected in making me feel entirely welcome and respected. Dr Sasaki came to the airport but, abashed by the newspaper stories, kept to the background. Instead I was royally greeted by the two young women who were to be our interpreters, Eri Ikeshita and Sabrina, two charming single girls in their mid-twenties, pretty, fashionably dressed. Eri, in particular, soon became more friend than interpreter and through her semi-Western semi-Japanese eyes (she had spent some time in the States) I learned a lot about the country.

With the girls at the airport was a good-looking stocky Japanese man driving his own silver-blue Mercedes. He was introduced to us as our escort, the man who was going to look after us during our stay. We were swept immediately into the centre of the city, to The New Otani Hotel where I found we had been put into the presidential suite, all marble and Empire furniture. Every room was filled with flowers and chocolates. Across the hall were the interpreters, the escort and a security man.

Soon after our arrival Eri came to ask whether I would mind being photographed in the gardens of the hotel. I could hardly refuse. The little photographer who dogged our footsteps in the coming days was the model of discretion and tact, and the reporter who tagged along served only to keep away the hordes of other journalists who would otherwise have plagued us. Next morning, a photograph of me, honoured foreign guest, took pride of place on the hotel board, alongside one of Julie Andrews, another recent arrival. Underneath was a lot of writing – in Japanese. I assumed it was a message of goodwill.

Now began four days of Japanese life as pleasurable as they were bizarre. My hosts were at pains to explain to me that all Tokyo was at my disposition, that I had merely to tell them where I wanted to go, whom I wanted to see, and when I wanted to do so and all would be arranged.

Searching around for a new project before leaving Ottawa, I had come up with the idea of bringing the set of cameras King Hussein had given me, and taking pictures to illustrate a Japanese cookbook. I have always loved Japanese food and thought that I would do a Western version of their cooking to help redeem some of my disastrous financial losses from *Beyond Reason*. When I told Dr Sasaki's team of my plans everyone was delighted. Within hours a schedule of restaurants, stores, and markets had been organized. Wherever I went, my photographer shadow and his reporter companion came with me. They were no trouble.

My job was due to begin my second evening in Tokyo. I had used some of the four-thousand-dollar advance to buy new clothes and I felt good. An electric blue Ungaro suit hung waiting in my cupboard, so I decided on that, together with the diamonds and sapphires I had brought with me from my personal collection of jewellery. I was ready, according to my instructions, by nine.

But then came a phone call from the club: delay your appearance, there are still too many people.

This was perplexing. Was I not here to *draw* people?

Just before eleven my guide escorted me to the famed discothèque. I had expected a Japanese Studio 54. I found myself instead in the elevator of a skyscraper in central Tokyo. We emerged on the seventh floor into a foyer bursting with press, through which I was hastily bustled, and into the sedate surroundings of a simple drinking club, like any one of fifteen thousand in the city. I asked about the music. No, my guide told me apologetically, Dr Sasaki had not secured the licence yet.

A number of Japanese dignitaries were waiting to greet me and I was placed on a sofa in the centre. After about half an hour of small talk, during which photographers from the hallway were allowed in to take pictures, I was told that my evening's appearance could now end. Nothing more was required of me. More puzzled than ever, I left.

Next day my Japanese escort, Eri, Janet, Sabrina, and I, together with our silent companions, did the rounds of

159

the Tokyo markets. I was entranced. Every day I was beginning to feel a little better.

That night, we dined at a restaurant famous for its blend of Japanese and French cooking. I ate tiny shrimps in a strawberry sauce, the like of which I have never tasted. Around ten I grew restless. What about my job? After all, I was here as a professional and I was determined to do it well. Eri reassured me: everything was going perfectly. My escort called to see whether they were ready for us. He came back with the words, "No, we'll wait a bit. There are still too many people. Let's give it another half-hour." He ordered another bottle of champagne while Janet did her best to soothe me: "For heaven's sake, just enjoy it," she said. "If they wanted it otherwise, they would say so."

For this second evening I had chosen my black Chloë dress with white lace, a relic from an earlier shopping spree. It hid my bulk, and once again I felt good. When we got to the club there were only a dozen people left. I was offered a drink, accepted a glass of Perrier water, and ten minutes later was told that I was now free to go.

Didn't they want me to talk to anyone? No, thank you, that was not necessary.

Dance, maybe?

Alas, we have no music.

Mystified, we left, our shadows in tow.

Next day, my hosts told me that Jun Ashida, Japan's foremost dress designer, wanted to present me with some clothes from his new collection. I was taken to his salon in the centre of the city, a stylish series of rooms in a small building of its own. I was photographed trying to squeeze myself into a white linen dress piped with black, which had its own jacket, and a black silk cocktail dress with red flowers. Janet was also presented with two dresses of her own.

On our return visit next day to collect our prizes I found that we had been timed to coincide with a visit by

Madame Ohira, the prime minister's wife. Since my visit could not be made official, the Japanese had found a way of honouring me discreetly, without fuss. Madame Ohira and I sipped tea in Ashida's salon.

This encounter could not have been more agreeable and did much to make me forget the shame of my first Japanese official event many years before in Tokyo in the autumn of 1976 when, frustrated beyond endurance by the strictures and coercions of officialdom, I had galloped up the stone steps of the Akasaka Palace between serried ranks of Japanese dignitaries, shouting at the top of my voice at Pierre, "Fuck you," only to see him vanish below me in an official motorcade.

Now Madame Ohira and I talked sedately of Canada and Japan, of the weather and clothes and children. It was all very delicate and pleasant and made me wonder somewhat ruefully why I had made such a fuss about conversations of this kind in the past.

That afternoon I was to do my one Japanese television appearance. Ashida had arranged for us to lunch at his salon and I was charmed to be introduced to the Japanese idea of a box lunch, which appeared in the shape of a lacquered black box filled with exquisitely presented delicacies, each in its own compartment. There was a morsel of spicey chicken in soya with ginger, a dish of vinegared rice with a fragment of raw fish, a tiny bottle of warm sake. Janet and I gobbled it all down.

The talk show could not have been more unlike *Good Morning America*. I was asked nothing that could embarrass me. Indeed I was scarcely asked anything at all. Did I like Japan? How many children did I have? Did I care for Japanese food? After each of my enthusiastic answers the interviewer beamed. Twelve million Japanese viewers, I felt, were beaming behind him. Not hard-hitting telejournalism, admittedly, but I enjoyed every minute of it.

Meanwhile my evening appearances went on, each

less taxing than the last. In fact, on the third evening, just when Janet and I were beginning to flag from exhaustion from all the splendid entertainment, we got a call from Dr Sasaki's office to say that there was no need at all for us to attend the club that night.

I made a feeble protest: was I *really* earning our keep?

Yes, yes, they all chorused. Certainly. It's all going beautifully. Eri had another batch of newspapers to show me: pictures of me examining the market, me eating in a restaurant, me buying toys in a Japanese shop. How could any one club, I wondered, go in for such publicity?

Next day I took my cameras along to a sushi restaurant – the raw fish specialties that are the best of Japanese cooking – and photographed the chef as he prepared dancing shrimps. Unfortunately I had to eat them too, which posed something of a problem since the essence of the dish is that the shrimps must still be alive as they slip down the throat. I did my best to drown them first in the soya sauce.

My visit was not all food and photography. I had two marvellous meals, one with eighty-year-old novelist Moishi Tanabe, who took me to a restaurant where they served little thinly cut slices of lobster and a house made of noodles containing a hidden treasure of fish. He flirted with me outrageously, telling me tales of Japanese life and holding my hand under the table, fully living up to his reputation of the Frank Harris of Japan. Then came a meeting with Dr Sasaki, which took place in a private dining room with another political journalist, all good talk and the friendly formality that so delights me in the Japanese.

At the end of the meal the guests slipped out tactfully while Dr Sasaki, who turned out to be charming, pressed an envelope containing the remaining sixteen thousand dollars into my hand and made a short speech. He thanked me for my help and told me how extremely valuable it had been in ensuring a successful launching for his new venture.

We both smiled warmly. I almost felt I should be giving him the sixteen thousand dollars: the five days in Tokyo had altered my life, transformed me from a lethargic and unhappy housewife, crushed into acquiescence by lithium, into a living person once again.

The next day was my last one in Japan. Shortly after breakfast Dr Sasaki called at The New Otani with his wife and two children to present me with a Ming vase. There was one for Janet too. I added it to my luggage, by now bulging with trophies, testament to the extreme generosity of my hosts. Everywhere I had been I had found myself showered with presents and my suitcases now looked like brochures for one of the immense Japanese stores. Even Mr Tanabe had pressed packages of porcelain, incense burners and gold paper clips into my hand.

As we were preparing to leave the hotel, full of regrets for I felt we could have stayed forever, there was a knock on my hotel room door. Outside stood Eri and behind her two perfectly dressed Japanese men.

"Excuse me, Mrs Trudeau," she said. "But these are two gentlemen who would like to ask a favour of you. It will only take two minutes."

I hesitated.

Her voice was slightly insistent. "I really think you should."

So I welcomed them in. The first turned out to be something of a man about town, a young man in a purple velvet jacket with hair down to his shoulders.

"Hi, Maggie," he said, with that easy colloquial American that so many young Japanese seem to master. "Have you had a good trip?"

"Well yes," I replied, "I certainly have."

"I would like to introduce you to my boss," he went

163

on, ushering in from behind him a pinstriped figure, all bows and smiles. I clearly looked surprised, for he continued:

"We're from the Cheval publishing company, and we have something to ask you. We're bringing out *Beyond Reason* over here this week, and we would like you to sign a message to act as frontispiece, something like: 'To all my Japanese friends, with best wishes, March 1980, The New Otani Hotel' and your signature. Then we'll paste it in the books."

Suddenly all was clear. The first-class tickets, The New Otani Hotel, the money, our shadow photographer and reporter. This was nothing other than a gigantic, all-embracing, saturation-coverage publicity trip for my book. Dr Sasaki and his little club were nothing but a front. I started to laugh.

"Oh you Japanese. You are so clever," I said, while my visitors looked a little disconcerted. And while I laughed it all fell into place. They knew, from press reports, that I would never agree to any more promotion for *Beyond Reason*. They had heard, too, that I was broke. What better way of drawing me to Japan than to pay me highly for a concocted job? Now, looking again at the papers and magazines that bore all the photographs of me, I saw that the captions all included what must be the title of *Beyond Reason* in Japanese. Oh yes, it was a brilliant ruse.

It was brilliant too, to have me escorted by such a prominant Japanese playboy, as I now realized my companion to be. For while the captions all spoke of me as an author, they left the impression that I was being courted by a Japanese bachelor and that I was relishing every minute of it. Nothing offensive or indelicate about it – just charming good manners.

I didn't care. It was the most effective and skillful promotion campaign of my life, and I had enjoyed every second of it. I left Tokyo a new person, for I knew now

164

with total certainty that I had rediscovered the strength to survive.

My four days as a working person again – if the pleasant hours I had spent on Dr Sasaki's payroll could be called work – had also given me a taste for employment. Settled once more in Ottawa, I turned my thoughts to a job. Twenty thousand dollars was a lot of money, but I still needed a great deal more to pay off my debts. What was I good at? Once again, my lawyer Cookie came to my rescue, even if his first idea was less than brilliant. He called one day and told me that he had arranged for me to launch the opening of a club in Montreal. I fondly imagined it would be like my experience in Tokyo. It was billed as an "evening of extravaganza and entertainment." It turned out to be a transvestite burlesque of the crudest and most embarrassing kind. I even ended up paying my own bills at the Ritz, where I stayed for the opening, because the management left town shortly afterward leaving its tab unpaid.

This fiasco was followed by a better interlude when I flew down to the Rockefeller Center in New York to take part in the TV programme *To Tell the Truth*, a game show in which the panelists have to identify, among several candidates, the one who is telling the truth. The producers record five half-hour shows all in one day, and then air them, one a day, for a week. A designer friend had lent me five outstanding outfits, which did a great deal for my morale. I returned to Canada very pleased and a little richer.

The money and the liveliness of the event went to my head, and I bravely agreed to follow it up with an appearance on *Big City Comedy*, a now-defunct Canadian show specializing in slapstick. Slightly intimidated at first by the sense of ridicule, I soon found that I could handle the comic turns and only blanched slightly when the final act ended with a pie being shoved into my face.

But television appearances, like most of my other enterprises, were doomed to end abruptly. In the autumn of 1980 I was invited to Nevada to take part in *Hollywood Squares*, the most stylish and entertaining of all the American game programmes. I checked into my hotel in Las Vegas with a stinking cold and awakened next morning, the day of my recording, to a knock on the door announcing breakfast. It dragged me from a tormenting dream of police and sirens. As my head cleared, I realized that the sirens were no dream, but a persistent wail beyond my room.

The waiter who brought my breakfast drew back the curtains to reveal a scene of science fiction horror: the entire facade of the building opposite, the MGM Grand casino hotel, was shrouded in thick black smoke, while helicopters hovered at its fringes like insects. I stood appalled, fascinated and terrified by the spreading flames. Soon a messenger arrived to take me to the studios, which were on another floor of my hotel.

Hollywood Squares is all about comedy. Participants are meant to be funny. That's what you're there for. While my hair was being brushed out and my makeup applied, I craned to see the television set in the corner of the studio. The fire in the casino was blazing ever stronger and now commentators, live at the scene, were beginning their litany of dead.

I was called to the stage. My role was to listen to questions put to me by a pair of guest contestants and to give witty replies. Clever, laugh-provoking cracks.

Between takes, I went back to freshen up my makeup and listen to still more news. "Here's body number forty-seven coming out on a stretcher. . . . Oh, look, there's a man right high up, perched on a window ledge. . . . Will he jump? Yes, yes, he has. . . . That makes forty-eight dead. . . . Now, that looks like a child up there, yes, it's definitely a child, clinging to his mother.... Will they jump?" Then back to more questions, more laughter, more jokes.

By the end of the day there were fifty-seven dead. The fire was out. But I felt destroyed. The contrasts of my day, death with humour, so sickened me that I could scarcely make it back to my room. I begged a seat on the first plane out of Las Vegas and fled the city.

That day of horror did something to me. It might have been a job like any other, had it not been for the fire. Those flames licking around the walls of the hotel gave me a jolt about my life. I started thinking about game shows and my own feelings toward such a chancy, tough way of earning a living. Did I really enjoy the second-rate glamour of those performances, slick on the surface, seedy underneath? Surely I wanted – I needed – real work, not make-believe?

After all, I asked myself as I put as many miles as I could between myself and the city, what was I getting out of it? Not that much money, certainly, though money to repay the interest payments on my loan was why I was doing it. Not much experience, since one was much like another, and I had already come to see that wit and instant repartee of the kind demanded of me on game shows were not my chief skills. Was any money or experience worth that sort of risk to my life? And what would happen to the boys if something happened to me? The fire had broken out in the MGM hotel; it might just as easily have been in my hotel, the Riviera. And so, flying home, I made a resolution. No more game television shows. At any price. I now refuse all offers of that kind.

Chapter Eleven
"What I Hear You Saying Is..."

The day before I left on my Japanese adventure, on March 3, 1980, Pierre and a thirty-two member cabinet were sworn in once more to office at Rideau Hall. Succeeding Canada's sixteenth prime minister, Joe Clark, Pierre became its fifteenth – reverting, according to tradition, to his previous number.

His victory had been complete. Two hundred and seventy-two days of exile had mellowed and humbled him into running the most successful election campaign of his life, and the results proved it: he got forty-four percent of the vote, only one percent less than in his 1968 heyday as philosopher-king of the young. Ontario was his. In Quebec he had every seat but one, a better performance than anyone since Mackenzie King's sweep in 1921. Only Western Canada stood out against him. The knowledge of his victory and the happiness I felt for him did much to prepare for my own extraordinarily successful visit to Japan.

On my way home to Ottawa, therefore, secure in the understanding that Pierre had no immediate need of me as comforter, I decided to stop off in Vancouver to visit my family and friends. So cheered was I by my Japanese visit that I also embarked on my first romance for many a long month. Travelling to Japan from Vancouver a week before, I had found myself sitting next to an extremely attractive American man. Six hours in the air is ample time to form a friendship. My companion, I discovered, was employed in installing communications satellites in Alaska. Before the trip was out he invited me to visit him there on my return, for a skiing holiday.

And so, braving my family's somewhat skeptical looks, I left my Japanese trophies at my parents' house in Vancouver and took off for the North. The bracing cold of Alaska, the unaccustomed physical effort of skiing, and the sheer delight in being loved once more all combined to make me believe in my own recovery.

On arriving home in Ottawa a couple of weeks later, I put all my suitcases on the living room floor, scattering everywhere the little ornaments brought back from Tokyo's amazing shops. I then sorted out my camera equipment and rolls of film for processing and storing, and thought no more about them. Next day I decided to take the boys for a treat to see *The Black Stallion*. We left home at seven and were back in the house by about nine.

I put the children to bed and went into my own bedroom, only to find a box of writing paper strewn all over the floor, and more disorder than even I was capable of. With irritation, I called up to the boys that they shouldn't make so much mess. Sacha called back, reproachful: "We haven't Mummy. We haven't been *near* your room." And then I looked more closely around me. Chaos indeed; and something far worse than the clutter of three small boys. Cupboards open; drawers pulled out; paper everywhere.

Instantly I realized that there must have been a burglary. I raced down the hall, gathered the children up and put them into my bed, closed the door and phoned the superintendant of the children's security force, preferring to let him decide how best to deal with it. My main fear was that the man might still be in the house, so

169

none of us moved until, seconds later, I heard the screeching of tires and whine of sirens.

It was then that I had time to take stock of the damage. Following the police, I now went back downstairs to the living room where I noticed what I had failed to see on my way in from the show: of my two cameras, seven lenses, movie camera and many rolls of film on Japanese food, all that was left was one meagre child's Instamatic. The suitcase with my presents was gone. The thief apparently had stuffed everything he could see into the case and carried it off. Farewell to my Japanese cookbook.

My jewellery was my next preoccupation. Over the years Pierre had presented me with many valuable and beautiful rings and brooches in diamonds and sapphires, one at the birth of each of my sons and many in between: these were sacred in my life, and even at the height of my anxieties about money I would never have dreamed of selling them. I now remembered with a sick feeling of terror that I had merely hidden the ones I took with me to Tokyo in a soft bag in the cupboard instead of returning them immediately to the safe. I flew to the cupboard, which I now saw had been completely ransacked, its contents torn from the hangers and shelves and heaped on the floor. But the little case was safe, hidden behind some old purses.

However, the thief had not been a fool. He had scorned the semi-precious pieces I had on my dressing table, extricating unerringly from among them two irreplaceable items: the Andrew Grima gold pin studded with diamonds that the Queen had given me on her visit in 1974, and a charming gold cross Pierre had commissioned for me one Christmas. Both had vanished.

There was one other blow, though I did not discover its full horror until later. My frantic inspection of the house took me to the hall, where I found my twenty-thousand-dollar fisher coat was missing. That was upsetting, but at least it was replaceable – or so I thought. I soon discovered that the insurance company with which I dealt had taken the usual "little lady doesn't need to be bothered with such things" line and failed to inform me that the company stipulated only certain items in the policy. So I got the full value of the cameras back but only one thousand dollars for the coat.

The children had been terrified by the event but soon bounced back when they were able to follow the police around the house with their fingerprinting kits. Sacha, as usual, took the most independent posture. The moment I had let him, he had torn off to his room to see whether the thief had stolen the golden butterfly I had brought him back from Japan, the pretty but worthless little paper clip Mr Tanabe had given me. He came back infinitely relieved. "At least he didn't get my butterfly. Because one day, that butterfly is going to make me rich." Micha wasn't a bit shocked, merely angry. It was the eldest, poor Justin, who suffered most. He couldn't believe what had happened and when it sank in he cried, as if all the innocence of the world had been destroyed.

The robbery had one unexpected result, and one for which I was extremely grateful. After I had moved away from Pierre and Pierre himself had left 24 Sussex, we had almost ceased having any police protection. While the boys were at Stornoway they had the services of a uniformed guard outside the house. Essentially it was a practical measure to stop tourists from storming the house. Now that Pierre was back in office he would once again be given a full complement of guards for himself and his sons, but where did that leave me? I didn't mind for myself, and would indeed have found guards an embarrassment, but I had been increasingly nervous about the vulnerability of the Prime Minister's sons during the time they were with me in my house.

Overnight all this changed. The police began by arranging for a police car to be constantly parked on a rotating system outside my front door, and I was given the additional protection of the embassy patrol, the squad that did the rounds of the diplomatic buildings every thirty minutes or so both day and night. The parked police car stayed there, of course, only as long as the boys were with me; when they went back to 24 Sussex, the car disappeared.

But the police really wanted to do more. Soon a specialist had appeared to scrutinize every vulnerable chink in the house. He proposed that iron grille grates be placed over the windows and that high barricades be erected around the garden, all of which I declined with passion, saying I could not conceivably be made to live in a fortress. I pointed out, with a certain touch of malicious pleasure, that it would hardly be right for us to emulate Richard Nixon, the ex-president of the United States who had ordered the police to build a Plexiglass windscreen around the swimming pool at his San Clemente home (he said it would protect him from a sniper in a boat out at sea). So we settled on locks and reinforced doors, and then I thought Pierre had rejected the plan outright because his office managed to misplace for many months the detailed police report presented to him for approval.

With John Lennon's murder, some time later, came a fresh sense of urgency about protecting the children. Fearing that the young man's attack on the famous pop star might be a feat others would try to copy – often when a spectacular crime has been committed it is immediately picked up and copied thoughout the world – the police now asked me to revert to the full security apparatus of former days, at least while the boys were with me. I didn't hesitate. I no longer felt wholly qualified to protect them myself from the sort of onslaught that might come our way.

Within days, we worked out a system. A police car takes us whenever we go out – and I have learned to appreciate the joys of not parking my own car and walking ten miles on a freezing day with three impatient boys. Police guards stay with us in stores and movies and each boy, if he is on his own, is guarded. Justin, for instance, skis on Saturday mornings away from the rest of the family, but he takes a guard from the children's squad along with him. At the same time, a series of special phones and alarm buttons has been installed in my house so that if there is a break-in, or attempted kidnapping, we only need to activate them to set off an alarm at the nearby police station. I have trained the boys to race for them if I am ever seized or in some way not able to get there myself.

All this, naturally, has had its effect on the children and not all of it has been good. Micha in particular is very anxious about robbers and talks constantly about what he will do when he catches them. Every time I leave the house he watches me closely to make sure that I have locked everything up properly. Not long ago we went for a walk down our one-way street in the wrong direction so that, to join us, our police escort car had to go back around the block. Micha was desperate with anxiety. Since he was dressed at the time in bright red sunglasses and it was raining heavily, I pointed out that no one would come for him as he was incognito. He was not mollified.

He is, however, safe. And it is not only our family that feels secure: the whole neighbourhood is now basking in a lower rate of crime than ever before, which may be just as well, since the chief penalty of our police ghosts is that they keep the car motor running perpetually when

173

parked outside the front door, for air-conditioning in summer, heat in winter, so that we live with the continual shuddering sound of the engine.

When Pierre and I had first parted, in the disastrous aftermath to my Rolling Stones escapade in Toronto just after Easter 1977, we had drafted a statement together about our intentions. "Pierre and Margaret Trudeau announce that, because of Margaret's wishes, they shall begin living separate and apart," it read. "Margaret relinquishes all privileges as the wife of the Prime Minister and wishes to leave the marriage and pursue an independent career. Pierre will have custody of their three sons, giving Margaret generous access to them."

This message, made in the fullness of guilt on my part, and intended only as a stopgap measure while Pierre was Prime Minister, was only taken by the public at the time as one more example of my perfidy as a mother. It seemed to clinch the image that I had abandoned the boys, that I had no further thoughts about their welfare. This was far from true, as I pointed out to an audience in Lethbridge, Alberta, not long ago, when I was speaking at a a local fund-raising event. "Our marriage had broken down," I explained after so many years of silence, to an audience more appreciative by the minute. "One of us had to go. I could hardly ask the Prime Minister to leave his official residence with me and his children left in charge." The people sitting in the rows before me laughed and cheered.

When I consented to give Pierre custody, on that terrible day in 1977, I had in fact made it perfectly plain that it was a very temporary solution. Pierre had agreed with me, but having the children under his wing had given him an inevitable superiority in the game, all the more so as they needed protection that I could not give them. I knew that it would be some time before I was sufficiently established to offer them any sort of alternative.

But now more than two years had passed. I had proved my stability as a mother, bought my own house and – as I thought at the time – secured my financial future by writing *Beyond Reason*. And so I embarked on a new campaign to share the boys with Pierre. It started when we both looked around and saw that there was actually no physical room in my house for Pierre and that the moment had come to explain to the boys that we were going to live, and share, separate lives. Before breaking to them what could only be traumatic news, Pierre and I decided to talk to a family counsellor, ask his advice about how best to present the information. Not that the boys seemed bothered. All three loved my house and, small as they were, had a real appreciation of just how much better Pierre and I were when apart from one another, and how much better we could then concentrate on each of them.

The family therapist, a rational pleasant man called Dr Melvyn Segal, was immediately helpful. We hadn't been talking long when he remarked, with surprise: "I can't fathom how you two could ever have been happy together as a married couple. Your personalities don't seem to me to be reconcilable." To my surprise, Pierre reacted openly to these sessions. Not that he was willing to explore his own personal feelings – that indeed would have been miraculous – but he was very prepared to discuss our marriage and what our attitude toward the children should be.

For myself, I found these sessions both comforting and enlightening, for I discovered that while Pierre and I had thought all along that we were really communicating with one another, we were not. Often while I was saying one thing he was hearing another. The new therapy technique was fascinating: I would say something, then Pierre would say something else, and then the counsellor would interject, "What I hear you saying is. . . ." We both would find it to be quite different from what we imagined.

These sessions did something else as well. They taught me a great deal about Pierre. As he skirted tentatively around the subject of our relationship, I began to see him emerge as a desperately lonely man (he chose to call it solitary) who had erected such an immense barrier between himself and the outside world that he was not really capable of a deep and trusting adult relationship. I was also touched by his appreciation of me as a mother, by how apparent it was that he actually liked the way I handled the boys. I, too, loved him as a parent. It agonized me to see our marriage come to an end, but I knew it was necessary.

And so the moment came to tell the boys. If we hadn't said anything before, it was simply that there had been no need to: what with my comings and goings, and Pierre's moves in and out of government, they had never seemed to notice anything peculiar about us. But now first I, and then Pierre, explained to them that we were very different people, with different tastes and ideas, and that we would be better off apart. Didn't Daddy like hiking and canoeing and art books? And Mummy going to bed late and watching television? Justin had long had a joke about Pierre being like Mr Spock, the Vulcan in *Star Trek*, the rational man with no emotion or frivolity, and we joked about that.

The boys took it well. Sacha, who is the most introverted, said firmly that he didn't want to have two Daddies, and Justin explained that he didn't want us to get divorced. Micha didn't say much: he just went on as he always has, full of chatter and jokes, like a scrappy,

176

tough little Sinclair. It was probably hardest for Justin, however, who got a couple of bloody noses defending my honour at school. But once the explanation for our separation was made, the boys became like all the other children at Rockcliffe Park Public School who have two parents' telephone numbers and addresses on the school list.

We had been to about six counselling sessions when the news came that Pierre was going to have to fight an election. The joint meetings stopped, but the political situation proved to be an unexpected bonus for me. Because he was away almost continuously for a couple of months, Pierre had no choice but to entrust the boys to my care. This gave him the chance to see how well I could now handle them, and also the time to accustom himself to a change of pattern.

When he was once again installed at 24 Sussex, while I continued to live fulltime in my house, we stopped and took stock. Neither of us was now in any doubt about a number of basics. To begin with, we loved and appreciated each other as parents. I in particular remembered with affection and respect the way that Pierre, as each boy was born, would cradle the baby in his arms and how soon a firm and loving bond was established between them. Pierre's role as father is vital to the children and is both rich and strong. While as people Pierre and I had not been able to solve our differences, we were nonetheless left with mutual agreement about values such as honesty and loyalty, education (that it should be bilingual) and behaviour (at least when it comes to manners and regular meals). Out of these strengths has come a way of life.

It began with a conversation between Pierre and myself. "What do you see happening now?" I asked him, shortly after he had moved back to 24 Sussex.

"Well," he replied, "I would like to see something of the boys during the week, but also on weekends, when I can take them up to Harrington."

I thought a bit. "I think the happiest time of my last six months has been the sound of their voices calling to me as they get home from school," I told him. "So I too would like a bit of school days. And I don't want to lose all weekends."

From this talk evolved the most natural and agreeable of arrangements. Because our two houses are three blocks apart, and the same school bus picks them up, there has been little disruption in the routine of their lives. We started by having them a week each, Monday to Monday, then switched to Friday to Friday, which gave the boys the opportunity to unwind over the weekend and be ready for a calmer entry into school on Monday morning.

The plan suits Pierre well. He keeps one nanny, who is on duty twenty-four hours a day for seven days, and then goes away for the week the children are with me. As for me, I'm chief cook and bottle-washer for my week with only the help of a cleaning lady on Wednesdays. But I don't mind. I keep my children's week bare of other plans and see my friends when I'm on my own.

And the boys? Each has adapted in his own way to a style of life that clearly is best for all of us. Micha, the baby, is the one who misses me most, but even he wouldn't change the way we do it; he makes up for my absences by calling me on the phone – at least five times each day. Sacha has become my house manager and bosses us all around when he is with me, telling me what I should or should not waste my money on. As for Justin, he takes everything in his stride.

The family counsellor made Pierre and me see how important it was, when it came to decisions about the children, to put our antagonism behind us and think

178

jointly about how best to handle their lives. And so we talk, perhaps as never before. There have been disagreements, but they have all been solved by talk and time, with compromises and a good many concessions from both of us.

There was, for instance, the question of the boys' education. Pierre, being a French Canadian, a product of the Jesuit educational system and a deeply cerebral man, wants his sons to have the finest academic tuition the country can provide. So do I – but not while they are small. I am a fierce believer in community schools and all three boys are happy at theirs, Rockcliffe Park. For a while, Pierre argued in favour of the school many of his friends' children attend: Lycée Claudel, a French private school out in the suburbs. I begged him to think about the importance of continuity, the fact the boys now have good friends, and to compare that to the rough and pressurized lives the Lycée Claudel pupils have to cope with. He thought about it, and came up with a suggestion I accepted.

The boys will stay at Rockcliffe until they are ten or eleven, and after that move into the French stream. If by then Pierre has moved to Montreal, this will mean they spend their weeks with him – but is that a bad thing? The English keep their sons in boarding schools with no ill effects, and would Pierre's environment not be a fine boarding school to be in? What is more, I am far from confident that I would make a better parent to them than Pierre during those awkward years of a boy's adolescence. So we are in full agreement over schooling.

The issue of sports took longer to sort out. Pierre is passionately averse to competitive games: he didn't like them himself, and he doesn't want his sons to play them. That made us see eye to eye on the subject of hockey, which I find violent and brutish (and what's more it entails getting up at six o'clock in the morning to get them to the right place on time). But I felt different about soccer, for which boys need strong legs and the desire to run, and which gives them the greatest fun. Pierre demurred. He said he wanted to take the children to Harrington Lake on Saturday mornings. He said he didn't want them playing games. But I kept at him, told him how important I thought it was that they turn into responsible teammates, and how I loved to hear them laugh and call out with pleasure at every goal. So he gave in to me.

That left the question of television. Pierre is not a television fan, or at least only a selective one, enjoying the late-night films on Fridays. There is no family television room at 24 Sussex, for the good reason that Pierre suspects that the rays are highly dangerous for little boys (he brandishes a report by some Spanish scientist to that effect whenever I bring up the subject). Both of us agreed early on, however, that we would not interfere with the parenting customs of the other. As a result, the boys soon became used to no television at home and a certain carefully limited amount with me, particularly on Saturday mornings, when cartoons grip every North American child for three hours.

Our Saturday mornings soon became a cozy ritual with us: every other morning the children had to eat some high protein cereal. On Saturdays they could have any junk food cereal they wanted, providing they got it themselves. Armed with this, they could stay in their pyjamas, wrap themselves in their quilts and perch in front of *Spider-Man* and *Bugs Bunny – Road-Runner*.

This arrangement went ahead smoothly for a while. Then the boys started to beg to stay over Saturday mornings with me when they were supposed to be with Pierre, and their begging became more and more insistent. Finally I went to Pierre. I explained to him how harmless I thought the cartoons were, and how happy they seemed to make the boys. He listened, reflected, and eventually agreed. Now the boys watch cartoons on Saturday mornings wherever they are, and there are no more long faces.

We were some months into this system of organizing our separate lives before I realized that what Pierre and I were trying to do was actually being done on a semi-official basis in several states of the U.S., particularly California. It is known as joint custody. The more I heard of the legal backup to it, the more impressed I was. I started doing a little research of my own. Anything to avoid the miserable and bitter battle of old-fashioned custody, the hideous acrimony of most divorces.

I learned that a system of post-divorce custody, involving no alimony but instead offering totally shared decisions on every aspect of a child's life, as well as shared time with the child, has been practised in California for more than ten years and is proving highly successful. No parent has greater rights than the other. The children from these arrangements, the evidence suggests, are emerging healthier, happier, more balanced.

In particular, I was struck by the tone and common sense, even dignity, of the clauses that can govern joint custody agreements: "The husband and wife acknowledge that their separation could do emotional harm to their children, therefore they undertake with one another that they shall at all times do everything necessary to ensure that the lives of the children are disrupted as little as possible," reads one. "They shall conscientiously respect the rights of one another regarding the children, they shall consider to instill in the children respect for both their parents and grandparents and neither the husband nor the wife shall by any act, omission or innuendo in any way tend or attempt to alienate the children from either parent. The children shall be taught to continue to love and respect their parents." And so on.

To me, the words come as a breakthrough. I have

181

sensed instinctively all along that this way of co-parenting is the right one; here it is enshrined in law. What is more, it is a generous solution, generous to everyone. Even while Pierre had the boys I knew that it would be basically unfair to try and get them away from him. Why should I, as mother, be *entitled* to them? They are his just as much as mine.

Pierre and I have not yet reached the stage of formal, legal phrasing, for we are not yet divorced, but I hope and believe that we are headed in that direction. I do not intend to seek alimony from him, and as soon as I get on my feet financially I will start paying my share of the bills for the children's education, clothes and health care. I intend that we share everything – every decision, every plan. Only then will we be joint parents in the best sense, mature and equal partners in a new family venture.

Chapter Twelve
Facing the Consequences

I woke up, one brilliant sunny morning in mid-May 1981, to see my world had changed. It had been changing all along, of course, but I hadn't noticed it. Now, suddenly, I realized how far I had travelled in two years, how much of the journey toward the right life for me had already been made.

It began with a phone call. I had been working for some months on this book and it was just about finished. I was pleased at the way it had gone, but doubtful still about how well it would turn out: was there anything more worth saying, simply about myself? My first caller was my publisher, Anna Porter, who wanted to tell me that my advance on the book had already been covered by offers for hardback sales and serialization rights. The news meant more to me than encouragement and success: it meant an end to financial worry. Now, at last, I could pay off my debts, stop looking for only the kind of work that brought in large fees, and start to plan for a real working future, taking jobs because I was interested in them, and not just because they paid well. I remembered the blaze in the MGM hotel in Las Vegas: no need, ever again, for those risks.

As I was sitting on my sunny porch, savouring the news, thinking of the improvements I would now be able to make to my house, admiring the way the petunias and the morning glories were coming up in the garden, the phone rang again. My second caller was Steve Martindale, my lawyer for the Paddington Press deal.

"Good news," he said at once. "Your Paddington Press worries may soon be over. The Marqusees have agreed to do their best to pay you what they owe you for *Beyond Reason*. They can't do it all at once, of course. But they have undertaken, in court, to pay back over the next ten years every dollar they owe."

Could I be hearing right?

Steve went on talking. "And remember the film script they did of *Beyond Reason*? The one that company took an option on? Well, they now want you to star in it. I have seen the script and it's a good one. They're offering a quarter of a million dollars."

This was too much to take in. I said that I would call him back.

The day's excitement was not over. Later in the morning, my mind still whirling from all this promised money, I heard from a friend in a major Canadian firm. There had long been talk of my involvement in a branch of Canadian industry. Now came a firm offer: nothing big, nothing very time-consuming, but a serious commitment. Something I had been hoping for.

All day, I mulled over the offers. By evening I had reached a conclusion. It had to do with more than money. It was about my whole life. I felt exhilarated, that sort of heady, breathless pleasure that comes from a certainty, an understanding about oneself.

First of all, I would turn down the offer to star in the film of my own book. Reflecting on it, I had decided that I didn't believe I could or should play myself: I would be too persnickety about the details if they weren't exactly right. More than that, I would find it very painful to keep

184

reliving a past I had now truly put behind me. And the glorious thing was: the money didn't matter. I don't have to look for superstar status and salary any longer.

Next, I decided that I would not only accept the Canadian industry offer, but I would probably take up one of the local television offers that had recently come my way. Two years ago I would have roared with laughter at the suggestion. My sights were on nothing less than *Good Morning America* and eight million viewers. Now I know, very calmly and clearly, that I need experience, confidence and a regular job. Then, my expectations and my fantasies were in full flight. There was no touching ground. Now there is. I no longer "expect" anything just because I'm Margaret Trudeau.

Early in 1981 I was asked to do a telethon for Ottawa's Civic Hospital on a local station, CJOH. I went along, did the show and enjoyed it. In May the same producer approached me again, this time to demonstrate some Japanese cookery in a half-hour show. The idea came out of a course of classes I had been teaching to eight women on Thursday evenings in Ottawa. It had turned out far better than I expected – it seems I have a surprising knack for teaching cooking, and since I love Japan I have been able to teach something about the country and the way the people live as well as the food.

After my televised demonstration, the producer called me to his office. "We have been talking things over here," he said. "Would you be interested in co-hosting one of our regular weekday shows, *Morning Magazine*, with Bill Luxton?"

I said I was definitely interested.

"But we have a problem," he went on. "Your salary. We can't offer you much, as we're just a small local station."

I thought hard. "Would you offer me the same as your

other hosts?" I asked. "I realize I don't have their television experience, but what I do have is my own experience of life."

The producer said that was fine. I told him that I would let him know.

And so now, on the evening of my apocalyptic day in May, I reached that conclusion as well. I would take up the CJOH offer. It would make me familiar with the world of everyday television, and perhaps eventually lead on to other things. And it would allow me to live in Ottawa, near the children, in the house I have come to love, and from which, when I get restless, I can make forays into the outside world, before hastening home to recuperate.

Hosting a television show will also answer one very essential requirement in my working life: immediacy and spontaneity. If there is one lesson about work that I have really learned in the past ten years, it is that I need tasks I can finish quickly. My great weakness is lack of staying power. It's no good asking me to think something through, and giving me a vague distant deadline to do it in. I need to see the end immediately. That's what I'm good at: reacting quickly, revving myself up and performing. Beyond that, I lose myself in doubts and procrastination.

In the course of my day of revelations I understood that I had come to a few other conclusions about myself. They weren't exactly startling, but they gave me some satisfaction. I see now that *Beyond Reason* was the account of someone beginning to grow up. *Consequences* is facing the reality of growing up, coming to terms with it, exploring its limitations: the last chapter, in fact. For ten years I had been put in a false position: I was supposed to represent a whole generation of flower children gone bad. Not just that, I was also expected to represent the problems modern women are facing when their marriages break down. All this against unbelievable public pressure and expectations.

I fully expect people to criticize me and say: you should have grown up, like most people, when you were twenty. But I don't think that there's any age limit to growing up. In my twenties I was just like so many others at that age: self-centred, indulgent, interested only in myself and my problems. I'm through with that now. I'm curious about other people. I want to involve myself in *their* lives, rather than be obsessed by my own. I'm sick of Margaret Trudeau's traumas. More than anything in the world. I want to get away from myself. And I think that now, at thirty-three, I'm ready to face real challenges, those related to me and my abilities and not to my position in society or my name.

Just as I can now accept criticism – at least from people I respect and care for. In the past two years I have developed a lot of confidence in people: I have learned at last the importance and joy of close friends. This discovery was an unexpected gift that came with my release from 24 Sussex and being the wife of the Prime Minister. When I married Pierre at the age of twenty-two the few close friends I had soon drifted away, unnerved by the grandeur of my life. Isolated behind the gates of 24 Sussex Drive I had no one to talk to. Now that I am no longer the wife of a prime minister, the people I meet behave naturally with me once more. The world seems a friendlier place.

Pierre often used to say to me: "Margaret, you must face the consequences of your actions. Your scatty, erratic behaviour is going to come back at you. You must take heed of what you do." Then I didn't really understand what he meant. Now I do, and I realize how much Pierre has helped me.

When I left him I was continually furious about his meanness over money. In retrospect I'm grateful to him for holding it back. Because had I had money I would never have struggled so hard to make my way, never have learned the lessons that I did about the value of money and life, and what it is to be a woman who has to make it on her own. I thank him for that.

I don't regret my marriage to Pierre. It was the best thing that ever happened to me. I still feel that I am his wife and that he is my husband. Not in the conventional sense, but I am proud to be the mother of his children. Sometimes I think I will never want a divorce or another marriage. I have a marriage already. If we couldn't make it work together, it's because thirty years separate us, a whole generation. Had we been closer in age, or not quite such absolute opposites in character, Pierre would not have judged me so harshly. Even so, I now find that I often cannot remember why we fought so hard, and for so long. I know only that we are friends once again, eager to spend time together, and that our sons are happy.

Justin is now nine, Sacha seven and Michel five. They are bright, cheerful boys who relish as much as I do the new life that I am making for us. We are learning, together, the four of us, how to grow. It is while watching them at play in my garden that I have come to realize how very ordinary I am, how very normal are my demands. I don't want the phony glamour and confusion of a Hollywood star. I don't want to be courted by playboys or followed around by the press. I want to work in my garden, be a good and constant mother to my children, cook good meals and work hard developing my career.

I also consciously want, for the first time in my life, to be physically fit and healthy (even if it's only to absorb all that good food and drink). I have found the perfect exercise in the form of the Nautilus programme, lifting positive and negative weights on a machine for fifteen minutes three times a week. I'm proud of my new muscles. It took me a long while to understand that my health is important.

A year ago, I met Jimmy Johnson. As children he and I lived for a time on the same street in Ottawa but we didn't know each other then. Like me, Jimmy is separated; like me, he has three children. He's a lawyer by training, a successful businessman by profession, a hard worker by temperament. He's also a terrific skier. We're about the same age and very alike. We have the same reactions to the world about us, the same hatred of organized functions and cocktail parties, the same sudden urges to catch a plane to New York or go to a rock concert. Jimmy is an easy and loving man and at times we look at each other and realize that we are thinking the same thoughts, not extraordinary thoughts or ambitions about power or politics – ordinary, domestic, unremarkable thoughts. We tell each other we'll get married when we're fifty, but meanwhile we'll be happy.

Sometimes I think that marriages ought to be like driving licences: you renew them if you can pass the test, every five years. Who knows if our relationship will last? We look at the future together, but in open terms, without too much desperation or dependency. We have both been burned, and we both know we can survive. It's a partial commitment, on certain selective levels, I suppose. For instance, neither of us wishes to act as a surrogate parent but we support each other over the children and don't interfere. We'll travel this way as long as we can.

The other day Pierre said to me: "Margaret, are you still bored?"

I looked at him in amazement. I had forgotten about boredom, the hideous, endless, crippling boredom of my life at 24 Sussex. Then I laughed. "I haven't time to be bored. Who could be bored when there is so much to do?"

That is precisely the point. I'm in control of my life

now, no longer the victim of other people's expectations and demands. I decide the food I eat, when I eat it and where I eat it. I choose the people I see and when to see them and where. I select my own books, my own pastimes, my own television programmes. Decisions come from me. I even decide my own financing now. One of the great burdens of the first months after I left Pierre was the tribe of agents and lawyers that preyed off me. Now I use them only when I need them for the law – no more being "handled" by anyone. My money is looked after by an accountant. For any other expert advice I consult the best person in the field, but only when I need him. I have learned to be very cautious of well-intentioned middlemen. Today I trust only professionals and my real friends.

I'm infinitely stronger as a person, no longer liable to be thrown this way and that by every passing wind. One of my great problems has always been my inability to say "no" to anyone. I grew up with an extraordinarily strong desire to please, accompanied by a total inability to let people down nicely. Now I have learned to think before I act, weighing the offers that come my way – people, friends, jobs, relationships. I take pleasure in a new-found ability to welcome those that are right and reject those that are not. I still make mistakes from time to time, for I continue to be optimistic by nature and tend to hope for the best, not assume the worst. But now, no matter how persuasive people are, I think carefully about the consequences of my actions. I remember Pierre's words.

Strangely enough, this sense of caution has come about not from a lack of faith in my own instincts but from a growing confidence in my abilities and a move in the direction of self-esteem. Haven't I written two books, acted in two films and done my share in bringing up three boys? Looking back over my marriage and my early days at 24 Sussex, I realize that I was continually plagued by self-doubt, a feeling of inadequacy and uncertainty about myself that was constantly exacerbated by my relationship with Pierre and the life that I felt I should be leading. Today that doubt has gone. I think I know where I am going and what matters to me, and with that certainty has come a healthy wariness about taking drugs and a proper understanding about how dangerous drugs like cocaine are to my system. I know, too, that whatever befalls me I shall survive. Through the painful failures of my life, I have learned one supreme lesson: when to exit. From relationships, parties, situations. I know when to call it quits. That's a great lesson of growing up.

Learning all this has been a painful business. I regret bitterly many of the things that I have done. I shall mind all my life that I robbed Pierre of his dignity at various stages of our life together by my unreasoned, hysterical outbursts. Pierre has more dignity than anyone I have ever met, but what I did was unpardonable. I feel ashamed of the way I used the public and the media to expiate my guilt and my troubles. I now know how wrong and foolish I was to blame other people for letting me down all the time, blaming them for not being what I expected them to be, punishing them for not living up to my illusions. I thought being the Prime Minister's wife was important. It isn't. What counts is being a complete person first and then tackling life out of your own strengths and weaknesses. It sounds so very obvious when I write about it this way – but getting to truly know myself was something I assumed I had already done.

I have also accepted that there are certain things about myself that are so ingrained there's no point in trying to deny them. I know, for example, that I like the limelight, attention, people watching me: I can't shy away from that. I like an audience. That is why I shall look to television and acting for my working future. But beyond that I know too that I want a healthy life stemming from a very strong base with no guilt and no self-delusions. That is my goal. In the confusion of my romantic youth I used to think that a goal like that put blinkers on people. I now know that to be absurd.

I thought my life of respectability and social standing would be over when I left Pierre, and I was terrified that I would spend the rest of my life as a social exile. I was wrong. As political analyst Richard Gwyn said in *The Northern Magus*, everyone accepts that I had to leave Pierre. It was the way I did it that was wrong. I'm sorry about that. But I'm grateful that I'm not an outcast, grateful to my friends, old and new, who have rallied around me.

Perhaps, in the end, all that I have done comes back to one simple fact: that I was not intended for political public life. None of it, not the people, nor the demands, nor the rules, nor even the rewards. They were not for me, and no matter how hard I tried, I could not shape my character to fit what was required of me. I don't like the world of politics and political power. It scares and bores me. Nor do I like the way it changes and controls the people who inhabit it. My escapades, my drug-taking, were no more than outbursts of despair at how profoundly I failed, wretched attempts to kick back at what I could not handle.

You have to pay a price for living someone else's dreams: that of your own needs, desires and independence. It was too high a price for me.